CHANNELLING

EVOLUTIONARY
EXERCISES
FOR
CHANNELS

VYWAMUS
CHANNELLED BY BARBARA BURNS

Light Technology Publishing
Sedona, Arizona

Published by
Light Technology Publishing
P.O. Box 1526
Sedona, AZ 86336

Copyright 1992 by Barbara Burns
ISBN 0-929385-35-7

Cover Art by
Johanna Heikens

Cover Design by
Elsa Gamaunt

Printed by
Mission Possible Commercial Printing
P.O. Box 1495
Sedona, AZ 86336

DEDICATION

This work is dedicated by the channel to Amo Tito of Moorea
and Lemuria and to the channels of
Moorea, French Polynesia.

CONTENTS

INTRODUCTION

Greetings, my dear friends. It is with great joy that I, Vywamus, connect with you.

For those of you who are not familiar with me, I would like to introduce myself. I am a being that you might think of as a Spiritual Teacher or Guide. That is to say, I am no longer present in physicality, but I have chosen to serve the Divine Plan by assisting those who are.

My particular focus at present, as it relates to the Earth and to humanity is largely as a teacher of channelling, for it is my belief that through channelling we on the Spiritual Plane may be able to assist and support you more directly as the Earth moves now into her next evolutionary step.

This work is intended for those of you who have made or are thinking of making a commitment to channelling in order to aid yourselves and the Earth. It is my hope that, through the discussion and channelling exercises that we are bringing you in this book, you will find greater strength, clarity and joy as you follow the path of service.

Let me say as well, that it is also my belief that all service within the Divine Plan begins quite properly with service to Self. As you look around your world, I am sure that you see many, many things that you deeply desire to change and heal. Some of these things, as I know you are aware, are not entirely, or at all, within your individual sphere of responsibility or power. This does not mean that you are helpless to heal the Earth.

I urge you to turn your attention, knowledge and dedication to that which you can heal – the Self. Look within and change that which needs to move there. As you do, I know that you will begin to see your world transform.

Perhaps it would help to see that this process can be compared to the actions of healthy cells in an ailing body that chooses to become healthy. Eventually they will exert an influence upon those cells around them, not by pressuring them to change, but simply through the contagious radiance of their joy and health.

It is to those dedicated healing cells
or beings within humanity that this
book is given.
✧
In love and Light,
Vywamus

CHAPTER 1
What Is Channelling?

Greetings, my dear friends. This work is a collection of exercises and commentaries on the subject of channelling. Perhaps the best way to begin is to discuss the subject of channelling itself. You know, many people ask me, "Vywamus, what is channelling and why should I get involved with it?" Sometimes they also ask me, "Why are you teachers so interested in channelling? You never used to be. It seems to us you never really came to us before about this, at least not that we can remember." Well you know, I think these are very good questions. I really appreciate the opportunity to answer them.

What is channelling? I think it is really very simple. In many ways, being a channel is like being an electrical transformer, those pieces of equipment you use to take one level of energy and step it up or down to another level of energy that is operating at a different vibrational frequency. You see, the great Plan of the Source as it relates to physicality involves many levels or dimensions of consciousness, wherein beings, similar to you and different, have their experiencing. As you are aware, the evolutionary Plan of the Source also involves movement from level to level upward ever more expansively. The energy from the Creative Core of the Source flows from level to level. Now, how do you suppose it gets from one level to the other? It is not simply poured out without order or focus. No. You see, everything within the Divine Plan, the whole structure, is based upon consciousness, consciousness serving the Plan and the Light.

EVOLUTIONARY EXERCISES for CHANNELS

The expressed energy, the Light of the Source, flows outward from the Creative Core by means of consciousness. All of us, as channels, help step that energy level down from one level to the next.

You see I, Vywamus, am a channel, and that is really one of the main things I do. My Soul's purposes or my Self purposes are very involved in consciously transmitting energy from higher frequencies. I bring it right through my own being and I step it down to a vibrational rate that is perhaps a little slower. When I am working with you and you are truly opening up to your greater consciousness in a more Cosmic way, I am able to bring to you knowledge, information, energy, love and Light from levels in which you are not yet consciously focused. Through my channelling these energies can come to you stepped down into an frequency that is more comfortable for you.

You see, as channels, you are all stepping the energy down from the highest level that you can reach right into the Earth and that is one of the most important reasons why you are in physicality. You are channelling from the Soul level, the Spiritual Plane, into the Earth where the Earth needs it to advance her evolutionary purposes and those of humanity.

Now, of course, everybody is a channel. You know quite well that, as a personality level expression, you are a creation of your Soul. The way your Soul has done this is by extending itself into physicality and channelling its life force into you. To do this it must step down its energy to a lower vibrational rate in order that you are able to integrate fully into the vibrational level of the Earth plane and thereby live comfortably in it. Channelling in one sense then is just bringing the life force from one level to another by means of your own energy format. You are doing it all the time while you are living and breathing here upon the planet. In that sense, everyone is a channel.

However, if you want to become a channel in a more conscious way, working and focusing in a more purposeful fashion, that is really what I, Vywamus, am here to assist you with. The focus now of our work is channelling from the Spiritual plane, where your Souls and the Spiritual Teachers, who are assisting the Earth's growth now function for the most part. From this level the Divine love and Light is brought down into physicality where humanity needs it. That is what I think channelling is.

Now this means that what you are dealing with when you are channelling is transmitting energy in a pure form. You can decide how you are going to utilize it. In what specialized ways are you going to channel this energy? Many people do this in the form of art, music and dance and that is a wondrous way of channelling. I really love channelling pure sound, for sound is so powerful and so moving. That is one of the reasons that I love voice channelling because the voice makes sounds. It is also a way that you can express the energy so that others can share it.

Now, of course, you know about channelling healing energy to assist yourselves and others to heal, balance and align their bodies. So you see, it is just really a question of how you decide to express or utilize the energy that you are transforming from one level to another.

As I have said, I am particularly fond of voice channelling because I love the effect that sound has. Sound is a very powerful creative element and it doesn't matter if you just bring it through by toning. That is a wondrous way of expressing energy and that is surely voice channelling, wouldn't you agree with me? However, sometimes it is very, very helpful to channel in a conceptual way and, of course, this requires the use of concepts and words to bring in the essence of an idea from the Spiritual Plane, conveying it in a coherent package of words and sentences that you can express with your voice to other people so that they can understand it.

How is that done? Well, I would say it is really very simple. You see, when you were a little child, you did not have any words at first, not that you could remember anyway. What you saw was a world full of shapes and colours and different kinds of energy. One of the very first energies you were able to recognize and put a word to was the energy of your mother. You found a word with the help of others that best expressed your sense of this energy and you also found words for the energy of your father and for colours and shapes and all kinds of other things. You even found words for things that you could not see such as heat and cold and happiness. You learned to find words for ideas, things, people and also for feelings and sensations.   As you travelled through your life, you gathered a wonderful collection of words to describe all kinds of experiencing and this word-assigning activity is a part of what your mental body does for you.

These words and concepts are available in your mental body and, as you grow up, you no longer have to think about what word matches a particular colour or shape. Right away the word "table" springs to mind when you see a table. You don't have to ask yourself to call up the word for table. When you see the colour red you don't have to stop and say, "Yes a colour, well, um, alright now mental body, give me the word for that particular colour. Oh red. Oh yes, thank you." You don't really do that, do you? No. It is very fast, very automatic and that is why voice channels who are somewhat experienced in using this talent for channelling can talk very flowingly and easily. They very effortlessly translate energy into words without having to think any more about it than you do when you see the colour red and say, "That is red." You see? It is not very hard at all. It is really just giving yourself permission and giving the Soul or Spiritual Teachers permission to use these skills that you have acquired.

Sometimes I think we should rename the process "word channelling" because it doesn't really matter for your own purposes if you translate the energy into words inside your heart and head without speaking and just hear them yourself. That is a wonderful way to have a moment to moment discussion with your Soul and Spiritual Teachers. It helps you to bring their support and guidance right into your daily life.   Sometimes, however, you want to share all the wonderful things that are coming through with others. You use the same word faculty that you have been using within your mind and heart, but this time you have to use the throat and voice to project it outward. It is not very different at all.

Now, I have often used the word "translate" when I speak about channelling and I would like to pause and consider that with you for a moment. In my view, this is what voice channelling is all about. You see, what you do is you take energy impulses and you turn them into words. You have heard, I am sure, about the method of communication called "Morse Code". That is the way people used to communicate in your recent past over long distances. Morse Code was really just energy that was expressed in terms of dots and dashes, or quick pulses and slow pulses. Now to me, that is pretty much the way the Spiritual Plane energy comes in through your channel before it's turned into words, like dots and dashes or energy pulses of different durations and intensity. If you went to school to learn Morse Code, what you really would be learning is how to turn those energy pulses into words. You would learn a language, wouldn't you? It is the language that allows you to translate energy pulses into words and it is truly not very difficult.

When learning word channelling, you don't even have to go to school because we are going to facilitate the process within your own minds and hearts, if you are willing. We will convert the energy pulses coming into your mind, heart and throat centre. We are just going to hook them right into that language ability that you learned as a little child. It is really very simple. You can just ask your mental body to allow the connection as you go through the exercise I will make available later in this writing. At first you might have to use your imagination a little, saying, "Well what does that energy feel like? What words seem quite right?" Don't worry. It will come very quickly.

Now the next question that you might ask is, "Why should I be a channel? What good is it to me?" I have already told you that it is a great service to humanity and to the Earth. At this time, many members of humanity cannot connect or believe they cannot connect (which is the same thing) into as high a vibrational frequency as you can when you are in channel. It is easy for you, really it is, to connect with your Soul and your Spiritual Teachers. Through you we can bring in very directly the wonderful Light and love of the Source to the heart of the Earth and to those of humanity who are willing to receive it. With the growth and changes humanity is going through right now this is greatly needed.

I can tell you that this is one very good reason for you to

channel, for it is one of the purposes for which you are here. You came and agreed to have a physical body and one of the reasons you did that is because the Earth needed your assistance in birthing a very unique and wondrous new species, homo sapiens. Of course, you came here to serve your own evolution, but, as in all cases within the Divine Plan, when you serve you are served. Consequently, a benefit for you in the channelling processes is that it helps you to have a very fine connection with the Earth, so that where you are, the Earth is assisted and humanity is more able to grow easily and joyously. I think that this is really an advantage, don't you? It would be nice if your relationship with the Earth and with other humans was more gentle and harmonious, wouldn't it?

How does channelling assist the evolution of Self? You did come here to evolve yourselves, you know. You really came because physicality is a training. It is like a school house that you choose to go to and you must graduate before you can go to the next step. There are many, many things that you need to learn before you take on more cosmic levels of responsibility in assisting the Source to evolve itself through Creation.

There is some wonderful training in physicality, indeed. If you are able to talk to your high Self, there is a great deal that you can do to enrich your stay in this realm because, you see, the Soul knows all the lives that you have lived, all the adventures that you have had, knows the lessons that you have learned and those you might have missed. Your Soul has, you might say, and "eagle's eye" overview of what is happening to you, of your relationships, your choices, your past and your options for the future. Sometimes when you are going through your life, you feel quite blind. It is a little like driving a car when perhaps you don't see well at night, for example. You don't see quite as clearly as you would like to and it gives you a sense of limitation, doesn't it? However, your Soul really sees from a higher perspective and is able to appreciate the whole of the path you are travelling on. It can see where you are on the path. It can see where you have come from and, yes friends, it can see the possible destinations that perhaps you cannot see with your physical or mental faculties. Wouldn't it be wonderful to have the Soul as your navigator? Wouldn't it be immensely helpful to be able to talk to your Soul and find out its perspective? I think you would feel as though you could see everything more clearly and would feel the security and joy of knowing that your choices are really taking you to that which is for your highest and best good as Divine being.

I know that sometimes as you are having your experiences, you get a sense of frustration and a feeling that you have missed the point. There was something there but it passed you by. I think that it is very helpful if you talk to your Soul of these things because the Soul sees very clearly what opportunities for growth there are in all your adventures and relationships. With its help you can see what truly is there for you. I think that through the Soul you have the ability to maximize your opportunities for growth and perhaps to utilize these opportunities in a more joyous way. You know that you can learn a lot by stubbing your toe or banging your head, but you could learn about the same things by being aware of what is there before you experience painful impact. So I think that involving the Soul in your daily life will help you to see the points of opportunity for growth and to move into them in a more joyous and easy fashion.

Now that is not to say that everything will be easy just because the Soul is involved for, truly, you still have a lot of responsibility for the appropriate action. You see, you can ask your Soul about something and your Soul can say, "Well you know I think that perhaps this opportunity could help us to see such and so, and I think that perhaps our best way of responding to it is to do this and that." However, you have free will. You don't have to listen to anything that the Soul says. You can say, "Well thank you very much, Soul. You are not down here and you don't understand at all and I think you should just leave this to me. I am not going to take your advice." Free will operates at every level, truly it does. Sometimes you don't involve the Soul as much or you find it rather difficult to stretch yourself to the level that the Soul says you are capable of. Always, it is your decision and your responsibility to act in accordance with what you view as the best choice for you. I believe that the channelling process is one of the most powerful and clear ways to get in touch with the Soul's ability to assist you with your choices. It is not a process which cuts off your responsibility or your freedom to govern your lives. It simply provides you with a much greater array of tools with which to do so.

There is another helpful aspect to channelling. One of the things I think that you are all asking for is for more support in your lives. I think that many of you feel a little isolated and not very supported sometimes when you are going through your challenges and your growing. Sometimes it feels lonely and painful. Other people seem to have their own problems to concern themselves with and you do not always feel entitled to call upon them. Truly, your friends in physicality are there to support you, and you them, but you also have a beautiful support system available to you on the Spiritual Plane. It begins with your Soul. The Source provided you with the Soul level to use as your direct connection into the Divine Creative Core. The Source knew that at times in physicality perhaps this might seem very far away to you. The Soul is always there for you, because it is you at a more comprehensive level. You know the Soul has created this and the other lives you have had in order to learn and evolve its understanding of its own Divine nature. At this point in its development, your presence on this physical planet is a very important key to its next step forward. Therefore, the Soul is always ready to pay attention to you, always there to support you, always loving and grateful towards you. It brings to you the Light and love of the Source. Don't you think you could use a little bit of that support in your life?

It is through the Soul that you get to link up with the Souls of other people. Yes, you have Soul friends, you do. These are friends who are in body and not in body, whose Souls are very dear and close to your Soul, often because of many wonderful adventures you have shared. These Souls are part of your support system and their personality expressions often are too if they are on the physical plane. As well, you link up with us, the Spiritual Teachers. Isn't that a wonderful support system? As you begin to more forward in your evolution, you really want to create your life in a more expansive and abundant way. The personality level support systems just don't seem to be adequate. They don't seem to be comprehensive or strong enough and they don't perhaps seem to be quite there for you when you want to really leap forward in your growth. So you need a vaster, brighter, more connective support system. I think that through channelling you may be able to make the conscious connections that will allow you to realize and to utilize moment to moment in a very practical way in your life the wonderful support system that the Creator put in place for you as part of the Divine plan.

Now the other question that I believe you might be asking is, "Why now? Why are the teachers coming to me now talking about channelling? Why did they not come before?" Well, there has been a certain amount of this kind of channelling on the Earth before. Many of you who are really drawn to channelling have had earlier training in other times. Perhaps you began in Atlantis or Lemuria or even before that, and certainly many of you had really quite sophisticated training in ancient Egypt. You really don't have to worry about how long it is going to take you to train in this life. I would say that most of you are really very ready. You have done all your training, most of it anyway, in other lives. However, it is true that there is a much greater emphasis on channelling now. I would say that in the last five to ten years we have really made a concerted push here on the Spiritual Plane. It has only been a few years that I myself have been directly involved in training channels here upon the Earth. That is because it is in some ways a bit of an experiment that we on the Spiritual Plane decided to try to see if we could assist you, and through you, the Earth and humanity a little more directly than we have been able to do in the past. So you might say that we have recently decided to try to utilize channelling more fully to accomplish our goals of service to the Earth and to aid you in your great service of helping this New Age to come forth on the Earth.

Through the channelling opportunity, we hope to be able to support the Earth and humanity more completely through the present changes so that we may move into all the new beginnings now emerging with flexibility and ease. You have heard quite a bit about how these impending changes are going to be accomplished by a lot of disaster and destruction. Disaster and destruction, from my perspective, really come when one cannot let go of the old without seeing it smashed or broken up. If one is able to let go of the old ways in a very flexible, joyous and adventuresome spirit, it is so much easier to bring in the new without disruption, isn't it? In your own life you have experienced at times that something was no longer appropriate for you. Perhaps it was a relationship, a job or something like that. You really knew that it was coming to an end and that it wasn't serving you very well. Oh, but it was so hard for you to let go and so you held on and you held on until everything fell apart. Perhaps the relationship blew up quite dramatically or you were fired from the job. Whatever it was just fell apart. That shows you that you can move forward and make changes in a more dramatic and impactful fashion. It's not so bad, because, in the end, the change still comes.

The New Age is going to come, my friends, one way or another, but won't it be wonderful if you are able to let go of the old when it no longer serves you and move into the new with a sense of joy, adventure and confidence? We would like that for all of humanity and for each of you individually as well. I think that channelling is one of the ways that we are going to achieve this. I, myself, have been watching very closely how the channelling has been affecting the growth and change of the Earth and humanity and I can tell you that I am delighted and that I really feel that what perhaps began as an experiment is a full-out success. That is why more and more Spiritual Teachers are coming more directly to those with whom they communicated with in the past in a less direct way. Many of you have been assisting the Divine Plan for the Earth in an unconscious way and it is channelling that can make this a conscious, loving partnership.

Now, many Spiritual Teachers are really deciding that channelling is the way they want to work with those with whom they are involved on the physical plane. I, myself, am giving lessons here on the Spiritual Plane to those Teachers who are getting excited about the channelling opportunity and how it is really helping them to carry out their service to the Earth in a more direct fashion. Many of them have come to me and said, "Well Vywamus, I really like the way things are going in your channelling classes with those wonderful human friends of yours. I too would like to utilize this opportunity. Will you please show me your methods and how I can work through someone in a physical body without my energy being very difficult or exhausting for them? How can I bring the truths from the Spiritual Plane to humanity without confusing or unduly disrupting the channels?" I am giving classes on the Spiritual Plane helping the Teachers utilize this wonderful opportunity so they can work with you in a gentler and easier way. I would say to you that this is why there has been so much recent attention to the channelling activity. Although it began as an experiment, I would say that from the channel's perspective, from the teacher's perspective and truly from the Earth's perspective it really has been a great success. We are therefore taking it to a deeper and broader level and that is why we are coming forth to you now in such an open and direct way.

I hope that I have answered your questions, dear Friends. I want to tell you that my mission has a lot to do with channelling. It is one of the most important things that I am doing. So if you decide that you would like to become a more active channel, a more conscious and knowing one, then I invite you to call upon me. You can just say, "Vywamus, I want to make a commitment to channelling. I really want to work with it. Come forth and help me." I can give you a visualization that might help. My energy structure is one that you might say is very encircling, very supportive. So when I am working with a channel, I like to create a bubble of energy all around them to encircle and support the channel's entire energy structure at all levels. I work very nicely with a sort of blue/violet energy. So if you wanted to see me in a visualization, you could imagine a great blue and violet sphere. If you like, you can give me a friendly face because I am a very friendly and loving being. If you want my assistance with your channelling just invoke me. You can bring me into your heart centre and even give me a place if you like.

I can help you with the energy of other Spiritual Teachers, as well. Perhaps if you are finding that you are making a good connection energy wise with your Spiritual Teacher but when the energy moves to the throat it is hard to bring it forth, I can help you strengthen the connection. If you call upon me, I will encircle you as the energy of the other Teacher comes in and I will blend my energy just a little so that everything is softer and easier and comes into your structure more smoothly and powerfully. Be assured that I will never do that without the agreement of your Soul and the other Spiritual Teachers and, most importantly, I will never connect into your space without your complete permission. We are really all working together - you, myself, your Soul and the other Spiritual Teachers. We are working for the Light, for the glorious unfoldment of the Earth and her remarkable new children, humanity. Truly, we are also working to aid your own evolution. Remember, when you serve, you are served. That is a great universal principle.

CHANNELLING EXERCISE 1
Meeting the Soul and Spiritual Teacher

I, Vymamus, am pleased that you have made this commitment to channelling and I can assure you that it is most appropriate at this time. Your Soul seeks to speak with you even more deeply than it has in the past. Please seat yourself comfortably, with feet or hips flat on the floor and spine straight. Go within. Please see that you are surrounded by a beautiful column of golden Light all around your body. The Light fills you and moves through you and you feel its beauty and its support for you. Now you become aware that this beautiful column of Light descends beneath you deep down, down into the Earth. This beautiful golden light descends down and down, farther and farther until it connects right into the heart of the Earth. You allow your conscious mind to gently descend down the column of Light - gliding, floating down the column of Light. As you descend, you see that it is bright and beautiful and there are no openings or breaks in the Light. It is strong and bright and clear. It supports you as you gently descend right to the bottom which is in the heart of the Earth. Now with your imagination, you see that in one hand you have five beautiful golden nails of Light and in the other hand you have a golden hammer. These are the symbols of your commitment to Earth and to the Light. With the strength and power of your commitment drive the nails into the bottom of the column so that they are firm and secure and strong, connecting your column of Light deeply into the heart of the Earth. Yes, your commitment is strong and bright my friend. You feel now a gentle, loving response from the Earth to your commitment in Light and you feel a beautiful golden/green energy flowing to you from the heart of the Earth.

This beautiful golden/green energy flows in to the bottom of your column of Light and it lifts you up in the column of Light. Gliding smoothly, cradled in this beautiful loving energy from the Earth you rise up, up the column of Light right back into your body and you feel the green/golden energy moving very gently but strongly through you. Now you look up and see that your beautiful column of Light goes up and up and up through the heavens, higher and higher than you can even see. You allow your mind, your consciousness to float up, up out of the top of your head, through the opening which is the crown chakra. Up you go, floating gently upwards in your column of beautiful golden Light and you look all around you and you see how strong, bright and clear is your golden column. There are no holes, no openings and you know within your heart that no one and nothing can come into your column of Light without your consent, for this is your place of Divine connection.

Now you move upwards more quickly, gliding up and up, higher and higher, and you see that there is a bright, white Light at the top of the column, so bright and clear it touches your heart deeply and you move with joy towards it. See the bright, white, sparkling Light that calls you and moves you.

You move up and up into the bright Light. You are floating high in this bright white Light of God, of the Source. You are cradled in the Light of the Source. You feel so large. You expand. Breathe deeply now, drawing in the bright white Light of the Source, filling yourself with the loving bright white Light. Now you see again that you have five golden nails in one hand and a beautiful golden hammer in the other hand and again these are the symbols of your commitment to the Source and to service of the Light. With the strength of your commitment to the Light, drive these golden nails right into the top of the column of Light so that in your imagination you can see that they are strongly anchoring this column of Light into the heart of the Source level, making a strong and powerful connection that will always be there for you.

When this is complete, begin to glide gently down, down the column of Light, floating, gliding in the Light, gently now. Looking around, see the beautiful column, strong and bright and clear and your heart fills with the joy of this Light and its power. Now you look down and you see your physical body sitting in the column of Light. You see the crown chakra is open like a great flower and you feel yourself gently sliding through the opening at the top of your head and settling comfortably into your body again. You feel now the bright Light you have brought with you filling that body, making it feel expanded and alive, full of Light.

Now imagine that your conscious mind is a tiny human figure of Light, standing in the middle of your head. Focus all of your attention into this little being of Light until you feel that you are this figure of Light within your head. Using your imagination, see that as you stand within the head, a beautiful stairway opens up before you going gently downward. It is a beautiful stairway of gold and white Light, sparkling brightly now, inviting, beautiful and clear.

You begin to walk down the stairs and, as you walk, they become brighter and brighter. There is a soft, gently, loving Light and it flows all around you as you move downward towards the area of your heart centre.

At the bottom of the stairs you come out into a beautiful room, a beautiful, large, well-lit room with high, high ceilings full of Light. It is so beautiful! Using your imagination now, see how you have furnished and made beautiful this lovely room. There are lights and beautiful colours. Perhaps there is furniture. Perhaps there is a fountain spilling out sparkling water with a lovely tinkling sound. You see with your imagination that all the beautiful things that you have seen and loved on your journey upon the Earth are gathered here in your heart. Yes, my friends, this beautiful place of Light is your heart centre. It is not just your physical heart centre but it is the centre of your heart energy, a great place which is the centre of your being here upon Earth. From this wondrous place you can go anywhere that you desire, for this great heart is connected to All That Is. Through the heart you are connected with all the wonders that God has created and to the Source itself.

Now my friends, you see that in one wall is a beautiful, large door. The door is beautifully carved and there is Light streaming around its edges. You feel your heart stirring as you see the brightness and you feel a great desire to see what is beyond this beautiful door of Light. So you cross the room and you stand before the door. You look closely and see that there is a sign upon the door and you can read the sign. It says, "This is the door to the Spiritual Plane." Now, my friends, with the strength of your commitment to Self, to your own growth as a being of Light, you open the door. Light streams all around you, beautiful white Light and a beautiful sound of singing that is high, bright and clear fills your ears. You can hear it in the distance. Now see that you are standing in a long, beautiful corridor of Light. You see far up ahead that at the top of the corridor there is more beautiful white Light that streams in and touches your heart, stirring you with joy and hope. You begin to walk up the corridor, seeing how beautiful it is. As you walk upwards the Light becomes brighter and brighter and the sweet high music you hear stirs your heart ever more deeply.

Now you come to the end of the hall and you step out upon a beautiful, wide, plane of Light. Using your imagination, you look all around you and everywhere you see Light. There are colours dancing and flowing in the Light. Each colour seems to have its own sound that sings and you feel it in your heart. You breathe deeply, drawing in the Light and the sweet, high energy of this place. You look around and you expand with joy, for you know the energy of this place. You have felt this in your heart before, but now it comes to you stronger and brighter than ever before.

You see far in the distance that there is a moving point of Light and that it is moving towards you. There is a golden path that comes right up to you and you see that a beautiful being of Light is hurrying towards you down the golden path. As it comes closer and closer, you use your imagination and you see that it is a great being of Light. There is Light flowing all around it and glorious colours trailing from it. Its energy is beautiful and strong and clear. It comes up the path and now stands before you. Using your imagination, give it a face. What kind of face would such a great being of love and Light have? Use you imagination and give it eyes that are deep and ancient and look into those eyes with your imagination and with your heart. You see an ancient wisdom that stirs your heart and you know that this one has been with you always.

You know within your heart that it is through this great

being that you came forth upon the Earth. Look deeply into those loving eyes. See how strong is the love there for you. This one is committed to you and loves you. Truly, you feel trust within your heart, for this one seeks only the highest and best for you as a child of Light. You feel the trust and your heart opens to this great being. Now the being holds out its arms. If you are willing, allow yourself to be embraced. Feel yourself surrounded with the love and Light and strength of this great being. Your heart opens and its beauty, its love, and its power flow through you, filling your heart. Your heart expands and fills with joy and yes, you know who this is. You know that this one is your Soul. You can feel this in your heart. Yes, you know the truth within your heart.

Feel how your heart resonates and calls to this great being. Your Soul looks at you and smiles deeply. It is seeking something, asking perhaps, "Do you have a place within your heart for me?" Perhaps you do. Perhaps you have been preparing all this time, making a place, a beautiful, glorious place within your heart for this wondrous Soul. If you are willing, guide your Soul to the corridor that you have come through. See how it follows you in joy. See how eager this lovely being of power and Light is to connect with you, to be with you, to speak with you, to communicate and be part of your life. Glide swiftly down that corridor, your Soul following you, and pass through the door back into your heart centre. See the Soul does not come in. It stands at the door respecting you, respecting your free will, your choice. It waits now. It waits for you to give it permission, to invite it into your heart. No one can come into your Light without your consent. Will you invite the Soul into your heart now? Yes, I think you will. Give now this invitation from your heart and ask your Soul to enter. See now how the Soul in joy flows into your heart centre.

Where is the place you have made for your Soul? Look around your heart centre for the perfect place you have prepared. Is it a beautiful chair? Perhaps it is a shrine or a crystal. Indeed my friends, you have long been preparing this place for your Soul. It is the reason why your heart centre is so beautiful. You have been awaiting the Soul. See now the place you have made for the Soul. It is so right. It is so beautiful and your love and commitment shines forth from the place you have prepared. Offer it to your Soul. See now the Soul in joy and delight takes up the place that you have prepared for it. See how perfectly you have prepared for the Soul. Now sit for awhile with your Soul in your heart centre. If you listen within yourself a message comes now from your Soul. You look deeply into its eyes, and using your imagination, you see that it is conveying to you a message of love and joy. It has waited long for this time. Listen with your heart as your Soul speaks to you now.

After you have communed with your Soul until this seems complete, notice that you begin to hear a gentle sound within the heart centre. There is a knocking at the door to the Spiritual Plane. There is great Light flowing around the door. Your Soul knows who is there. It is someone from the Spiritual Plane seeking to connect and speak with you. Your Soul smiles at you, for it knows the great and loving being that stands awaiting you in your corridor to the Spiritual Plane. Will you go and see? Your Soul and you go to the door. Your Soul smiles at you, reassuring you that truly this one who comes, is in the Light, is a great and loving being. It is a Spiritual Teacher, perhaps a Master that you have worked with before, my friend, one that you have loved and known. Now will you open the door? I think so. Your Soul encourages you.

See yourself opening the door. There is a great being of Light standing there, respectfully. It is a Teacher from the Spiritual Plane. It does not come in because you have not yet invited it, not yet given permission. Look closely at this wondrous being. At first you only see a great body of Light. Now, use your imagination. What kind of face would such a great being of Light have? Give it such a face. Perhaps your secret memories will show you how that wondrous one was dressed and looked the last time you connected with it clearly. Who is this great being of Light? You look deeply into its eyes and ask. It will tell you. If you have difficulty receiving this information, listen with your heart and you will know. This Spiritual Teacher now seeks to connect with you again, to work with you in service to the Light. This one asks your permission to step into your heart to communicate with you. Perhaps you will allow this one to enter. I think you will, my friend, for a part of you knows this one very well. See now as you give permission, this beautiful being of Light enters into your heart centre, filling your heart with its loving, bright energy.

As you connect with it, you feel a deep trust and recognition. Truly, you know that this connection is from the Light, from the Source. If you listen very deeply, there is a message in your heart from this great Teacher. If you listen, your heart will tell you what the message is. Listen to the message of love and wisdom that is being given to you. Pause now and take a little time to commune in your heart with your Spiritual Teacher. I believe there is also a message for you that this Teacher will return to your heart centre again if you will but invoke and invite.

When you feel complete with this communication, gently release the connection. The Spiritual Teacher embraces you lovingly and departs, but you feel that some of the beautiful Light and energy still remains with you in your heart, giving you support, hope and love. Now rest within your heart, *enjoying the company, Light and love of your Soul, feeling the Soul's energy expanding and filling your heart. Now my friend, begin to release the energy that you have been channelling. Begin to feel the energy releasing above your head and flowing down the top of your head, and running like water from the neck and shoulders down the back and chest, like water running away in the sand, ebbing gently, flowing away. It moves down your body down into the root chakra and moves down through the legs and feet, flowing down into the Earth. You release this bright beauteous energy that has been flowing in your column of Light into the Earth. As that Light that you have channelled touches the heart of the Earth, you feel again the loving response of the Earth and a beautiful green energy sparkling with gold comes flowing up from the heart of the Earth into your body. It flows up, filling your body gently, softly, nurturing and supporting you. This beautiful green/golden Earth energy flows right through you and out the top of your head, moving up the column of Light and into the glorious white Light of the Source at the very top of your column. You see my friend, the Earth and the Source connect and embrace through you. Through your channel you connect them in love and Light. It is a great service that you do in this way.*

Rest now in your column of Light in the heart centre. Feel yourself cradled gently in the energy of your Soul and the Earth. When you are ready, feel your consciousness filling up your body, your arms, your legs, your pelvis, your back, your chest, your neck, your head. You are fully occupying your body now. You are centred strongly and balanced firmly within your physical structure. Rest now and when you are ready, open your eyes.

CHAPTER 2

The Nature Of Communication

In this chapter we are going to talk about relationships. When I speak of relationships, the first thing you think of is relationships between yourself and other people, but that is not the full story. You see, a relationship is any kind of connection between two points of consciousness. For example, when you hold a crystal, which is a representative of the mineral kingdom, you can really feel its life force. All life has consciousness. Perhaps it is not self consciousness like yours, but nevertheless, life is consciousness. When two points of consciousness connect with each other, they have a relationship. Every time consciousness touches consciousness and interacts in any way, there is a relationship. This broadens our discussion on relationships a lot, doesn't it? You have, for example, a relationship with the Earth. You have many relationships with members of the mineral kingdom, the plant kingdom and the animal kingdom. For example, if you have a little pet, you have a relationship between two points of consciousness. When you are working with a Spiritual Teacher, you have another relationship between two points of consciousness. If you are so open and loving a being that you have connections or communication with the Devas, these are relationships too. The term "relationship" covers a lot of ground.

How is a relationship created and continued? Essentially, I would say, that it is through communication. When two points of consciousness get together and experience each other, what is really happening is that they are sharing their space and they are transferring energy between them. So a relationship is perhaps best described as an energy exchange through communication. This is why channelling is so very useful in relationships. It helps you to understand in a very focused and knowing way what it is that you are exchanging with another being. For example, when we channel and teach channelling most of you say, "Oh I was doing that already. I didn't realize that was channelling." What we have been teaching is how to do it in a focused and purposeful fashion so that you know moment to moment who you are sharing what with. When you get together in a group to channel, much is communicated and understood. Afterwards you all talk about it, and anything you might have perhaps forgotten begins to come forward, so that after an evening spent together talking to your Spiritual Teachers you go home and you have a very good idea what kind of communication you were involved in. What we are doing is making your communication more focused and more conscious. Now I really am going to focus my discussion on relationships with other people, but I wanted to make sure that you understand that what we are talking about applies to any exchange of energy between two points of consciousness.

A lot of communication and, therefore relationships, are not very conscious here on the Earth. I think you are all discovering that you communicate with other people all the time in ways that you are not even aware of. You are coming to understand here what body language is and you are also beginning to understand what auric fields are. Many of you understand very well that people's energy talks to you and tells you what they are feeling and tells you the state of their health as well. You are all becoming very aware of certain communications and relationships that you have had with other people on a very subconscious or subliminal level. It is very important to start bringing those communications up into a purposeful, conscious and focused level the way we are doing with the channelling process. You are often communicating a lot to another person that you don't know you are communicating and they are respond-ing to the communication that you have unconsciously given. Some-times the way others respond to you seems quite strange. For example, when you come into a room at a social occasion, you do not always know why some people seem to respond to you so warmly when they have never met you before and why other people seem to take a delight in being annoying when you have also never met them before that you know of.

I would like to tell you that as you come into that room you are already communicating. You have been communicating for a long time in this life and in other lives on a number of different levels. This is where it gets interesting. The only communication level that most people on the Earth are aware of is from the personality ego level of Self to the personality ego level of another. Most of you are quite aware that you have other focuses. You have a physical body, an emotional body, a mental body, a spiritual body and a Soul, for example, and there are other focuses of Self that you may not yet be aware of. Did you know that when you are relating to another consciousness you are speaking or communicating at all levels? You know about body language. That is a beginning for understanding the ways in which your physical body speaks to the physical body of another person. You are also beginning to understand, as you be-come more and more aware of the way other people feel to you, that even the physical body is sending out other messages that are not visible to the eye. You know when you are near a person whose body is in overdrive, although they are not necessarily saying anything, at a certain level you are feeling the knots in their muscles and the way their nerves are jangled. You are getting physical communication.

As well, you communicate a lot at an emotional level. Even on the Earth now, people are beginning to understand that and some-times when they do, they talk about taking on another person's emotional "stuff". You have experienced this when you go into a room and there is someone who is very depressed. At first, because you are so cheerful, you try to cheer them up but all the time their emotional body is talking to yours, perhaps telling yours how depressing everything is. If your emotional body is not feeling very powerful, it sometimes says, "You know you are right. It really is awful isn't it? I know what you mean. Just the other day I was feeling that very thing." All of this is going on quite below the notice of the personality ego level. All you have been accustomed to registering is that for some unknown reason you begin to feel depressed.

Mental communication is also becoming well known upon the Earth. You have all heard of telepathy. Well, there is quite a lot more to it. The mental bodies of people communicate on an ongoing basis, often without any conscious awareness. They send thoughts back and forth all the time while the personality ego doesn't hear a thing. The kind of thoughts that sometimes go back and forth are things like, "Here comes that really annoying person again. You know if I wasn't such a gentleman I would tell him what I really think", or, "Here comes that whiny person again. I wish she would be quiet for goodness sake." Did you know that the person's mental body gets the message pretty clearly? They send something back which is often just as abrasive, for obvious reasons. While all this is going on, often the personality ego is saying aloud, "Oh it's so good to see you again. It's just been ages. I was just saying to myself the other day, where is my good friend so and so?"

What is really happening? With all of these different levels of communications going on mostly unacknowledged, there is a confusion that sets in. Many of you have had the experience of knowing people that are very nice to you and go out of their way all the time and yet you never feel very grateful to them. Sometimes it's because their mental body is saying, "I give and give and give to that ungrateful person and they never give anything back. They are lucky to have a friend like me. They are very fortunate that I like them at all"; and your mental body is saying, "As far as I am concerned you can just keep your begrudging niceness." At a conscious level you just smile and say, "Oh thank you for that lovely gift. I really appreciate it. You do so many wonderful things for me." Then you both go off feeling very uncomfortable. While you have been having very contradictory communications at different levels, you are only aware of the personality level interaction which does not seem to be consistent with your uncomfortable feelings.

Of course, your spiritual bodies communicate too when they become developed enough to talk to each other. This is usually not in the early stages of evolution in physicality. At that stage there isn't a great deal of communication at this level. When a being reaches the evolutionary stage that you have, the spiritual body becomes quite expanded, normally about a foot and a half or more beyond the physical structure, and some are quite a bit larger. When you gather together in groups to meditate and channel, your spiritual bodies become very activated and aware of incoming energies. They interact very enthusiastically with each other and with the Spiritual Teachers. This excitement and joy is most often felt by you as a sense of expansiveness and purposefulness.

When Souls evolve, their ability to communicate evolves. We can look at Soul level communication as well. I think you know that Souls talk to each other all the time on their level. I find that they are quite talkative, because they love to relate and communicate and they know each other very well. It is so easy to get a Soul talking. They love to communicate. Why do Souls like to communicate so much? Well, there are two good reasons I can think of. One is because Souls are at a level of consciousness where they are able to see quite clearly that we are all part of the same Wholeness, and that talking to each other helps us to experience the Oneness. This is very much the purpose for the heart centre "Boardroom" exercise I will be giving in the next chapter. The goal in that exercise is to have all parts of your consciousness communicate so much together that after a while they don't seem to be separate any more. They all begin to recognize that they are part of the whole that is Self. Experience of the Oneness comes through communication. As I view it, this is the thrust of our Divine Plan. Ideally, the sparks of life that flow from the Source are always recognizing each other in their totality through loving communication.

There is another reason why Souls love to communicate and that is because that's the way you evolve. Think about that. How is it that evolution comes through communication? Well, we know that evolution seems to come from having experiences. What has that got to do with communication? Well, an experience is a communication. Perhaps you are having an experience with another person, with the planet, with a consciousness from another Earth kingdom or with a being from a plane of consciousness quite beyond the Earth. Having an experience is just taking your energy and connecting it with the energy of these beings, places and events, all of which have consciousness moving within them because they are alive with the life force of the Source. If you were to put yourself in a little box, where there was absolutely no other consciousness to interact with you, I think it would stunt your growth a little in terms of evolution because you would have no experiences to challenge and expand you.

I like to talk about the patterning, the communicative patterning that is really, for me, what the Source Plan is all about. The Plan I am always talking about is a series of multi-levelled progressions of communication. The Plan is one great network of living consciousness communicating and interacting through their communications. Communication is the method the Source has chosen to evolve Itself, and you, being part of the Source, evolve your Self through your communications. Now that shows us how important communication is, because if your evolution depends upon communication, I think it is probably something you will want to do very well.

You know that on the Earth there are many opportunities to communicate in ways that aren't very much fun. You know that if you have an argument with your neighbour and you start throwing rocks at each other that is not a communication that makes you feel as if you are evolving very much. When you try to relate to other people and they seem to want to block you everywhere you turn, that doesn't feel very evolving - at least not until you are through with it. I think all of you are saying to yourself, "I wish that other people would not try to get in my way so much. I wish people would understand who I truly am and treat me with love and respect." Sometimes you are saying, "I wish people would not communicate with me at all in those dreadful ways. If that's the only way that they can communicate I would like them to go away." When you think that communication is every kind of contact between points of consciousness, I think you would say that many of the frustrations in your life have to do with inadequate communication.

I have a suggestion. I would like to say to you that, from my observations, the method of communication that is generally taught on the Earth is from ego personality to ego personality. I think it is probably the most inefficient level of communication available. I think that's one of the biggest reasons why you are not very happy with your communication. When I look at all the levels of communication that are possible, I think that the Soul level of communication is perhaps the most satisfying. One of the reasons is because Souls don't hide anything. Souls don't have any secrets. Why would you hide anything from anyone? There is only one reason I can think of and that is fear. If you think about all the things you do not want people to ever know about you, I think you will agree that fear is behind this, fear that people will do something to you if they find out, fear that they will take advantage of you, fear that they will laugh at you or that they will reject you. Really, secrets are all based on fear. Souls don't have that much fear I have noticed, so they don't have many secrets. They are very open and loving and enjoy communication greatly. They tell the truth, always. Sometimes you do not understand exactly what they are communicating and what they are saying but believe me, they are trying to give you the truth as they view it from their level.

There is something else about Souls that I really like. They are always loving. Even when they have to tell you a truth that might seem a little sour, they do it in the nicest way, right from the heart. Souls are full of Light, so they never give you darkness when they connect with you. I would say that when you think about the things you do not like about your communications and therefore your relationships, I think you will find that the solutions are to be found in Soul to Soul communications. What I recommend to solve this problem of relationships is that you get to know the Souls of people you are dealing with. How do you suppose you go about that? Well, since your Soul is a very good friend of the other Souls that it connects with and since you are getting to be quite communicative with your Soul, I think that your Soul would be able to arrange a higher level of interaction between you and others. It's like seeing a wonderful person at a party and knowing that you really want to talk to them but you believe that you don't know them. You have to find a mutual friend who will make the introductions for you. Then your communication will go very well. So what we do is to just ask your Soul to make the introduction. It works very well.

I think some of you might be saying to yourself, "Well, that's very nice but my problems with these people are down here, not up there. I am pretty sure that if I got up there I would like them quite well, but that's not the situation right now." As a channel, you are able to bring the higher vibrational truths and anchor them in your daily life. You bring the information, the understanding, the tolerance and compassion from the Soul level right down through the dimensions. As you know, this actually involves the assistance of your four bodies. If they are all aligned with the Soul they are quite agreeable to bringing the Soul level truth into their actions and communications.

When all the focuses of Self really agree and get into a complete alignment with the Soul about your relationships with others, Self as a whole begins to send out only one message to other people. Physically, emotionally, mentally and spiritually you are communicating the same Soul inspired message. After a while, people begin to think that you are a very, very focused and clear person. Did you ever wonder why sometimes a perfectly good idea isn't very convincing to other people? Often this is because part of you might be telling them another story. When you are saying the same thing to people at all levels they really receive the message, and if it is a message that is coming from the very highest level, it is a high, clear, loving, life-filled truth that doesn't bring back attack, scorn or rejection. Once in a while you draw a blank, but that's because the personality level just doesn't know how to respond to the truth that their Soul has communicated to you through your Soul.

I believe that communication with the Soul level makes it very easy for you to be compassionate, loving and tolerant with others, even at the ego personality level. Sometimes a person's Soul tells you something about them that you did not know, which makes you feel very compassionate, and you better understand those annoying things they do that have previously upset you. Sometimes you treat other people in a particular way because you are very sure of who they are and the reasons for their behaviour. If you talk to their Soul you may come to realize that you never really understood their feelings and their view of their own reality. Often, once you do this it is easy to empathize, to put yourself in their shoes and to feel compassion. Sometimes you think people are attacking you and they keep acting that way and you want to attack them too. Then you find out from their Soul that they act like that because they are afraid and lonely, and this is their idea of how to deal with that. Well, you no longer feel like attacking them. Sometimes you feel like shaking them and saying, "Look this is no way to get my affection," but nevertheless, you understand and you are no longer triggered into automatic responses over and over again with these people.

The process is really very easy. It is much like getting your Soul to be the operator on the telephone. You dial a number and your Soul makes the connection with the Soul of the other person.

As you remember from our other discussions, the strength of your will or intention is very, very important and it is really quite easy to focus your intention. Sometimes a statement made very clearly in your mind is just what you need. What I would like you to do now is pick a person with whom you would like to have clear and effective communication. Perhaps it would be more interesting if it were a person with whom you cannot communicate well face to face. This exercise is perhaps the most useful when you can't talk to the person very effectively at the personality level. It is also appropriate to pick the subject about which you want to communicate. Remember, when you talk to the Soul of the other person, it is not going to have any conflicts with you. This is going to be surprising for some people. Despite the fact that there may be a lot of hostility activated at the personality level, the interaction at the Soul level is very loving. Souls always love each other. So if you are dealing with a very hostile personality level, don't expect to see a hostile Soul, because you won't. Remember, in this exercise when you are communicating that it is the personality ego level on the Earth plane that you are having the difficulty with, not the Soul. Remember these are two very different levels of consciousness.

There is one more thing that I want to remind you about before we begin this exercise. You know that when there is a difficulty in a communication it is never only one person's responsibility and I think you will have to agree that you are probably doing something that is fostering or at least supporting this lack of communication. Of course, it is your personality ego level that is doing this, certainly not your Soul. When you are engaged in a difficult communication, it is important that both parties come from the highest level. Remember that you are going to be speaking to that other Soul through your Soul and if you start getting angry or irritated, you are in your personality level. If you start to feel the irritation or anything that feels heavy or dense, pull yourself up and say within yourself, "Soul, help me now, I am losing our connection a little." Then imagine that you are wrapping yourself in the Soul Light and move yourself to the higher level of consciousness.

I know that you are the kind of person that takes responsibility for your communications and relationships. Otherwise, you would be approaching this issue of communication from your personality level, saying, "I am doing everything properly. I can speak for myself. I don't even have to talk to my Soul. I have got it all right. It's only the other person that is wrong"; but you really do understand that you are quite causal in your difficult communications.

CHANNELLING EXERCISE II
Soul to Soul Communication

Make yourself comfortable now. Begin by putting your column of Light all around you. Of course it is already there. Have you noticed that? It is always there. When we say "Put it up around you," we really are not being accurate, are we? What I am saying to you is, "Notice that your column of Light is all around you." It is below your feet touching into the heart of the Earth. It is above your head, connecting with the Source level. It is huge, bright and unbroken and it is all around you. See yourself going down those wonderful stairs from the centre of your head right into your heart centre. The heart centre is that magnificent place from which we will begin all of our exercises, for it truly is your point of connection with All That Is. Please make now a strong, clear, focused statement of purpose, specifying the person you want to communicate with and the purpose of that communication.

When this is complete, gather all of Self into the Soul energy. It is important that you connect well with the Soul. I suggest that you see yourself flowing right into the Soul, and becoming wrapped all around with the Light of the Soul, just as if you are wearing the Light of the Soul like a great robe. See a door in one of the walls in the heart centre. You see that this is the door you have discovered before, the door that says, "This is the Door to the Spiritual Plane." Open that door when you are ready. By this time, you are very familiar with the wonderful corridor that goes up and up, towards the Light and you go up that corridor so easily now. It is really very familiar. You go up and out onto the Spiritual Plane, which is broad and bright and full of Light. I think it would be a good idea if you would call one of the Spiritual Teachers, because often we can be very helpful in assisting you as you work with these energy exercises. Call or invoke one the Spiritual Teachers that you enjoy working with, and using your imagination, see that this Teacher is now coming up the path towards you, greeting and waving at you. We are very supportive of high level communications.

As is the case with all of the exercises I am giving you in this work, this is a channelling exercise. You must give all the points of consciousness involved words with which to express themselves. Ask your Soul to call the Soul of the person with whom you want to speak. See that you Soul begins to make a vibration. For some of you, you will actually hear a Soul tone or note. It is really a vibration. It is like a name but it is a sound. So your Soul is calling the name or vibration of the other person's Soul, calling brightly and clearly. The vibration echoes across the Spiritual Plane and now, there is response. There is another sound or vibration that comes from the distance, answering your Soul. It is a bright, beautiful and clear sound. It is a wonderful being that is responding. Of course, it is the Soul of that other person. Now you see a bright Light hurrying towards you along a golden path just the way your Soul came to you when you first began to work with it.

You sense that the two Souls are communicating in sound and vibration. It is very much like a conversation of two dear friends who perhaps have not seen each other for a day or so and are greeting each other and saying, "How have you been since I saw you yesterday?" The other Soul may be saying, "Well, my goodness, who do you have with you?" Perhaps your Soul is saying, "This is my personality level. I am very proud of this one. It has come to talk to you about a difficulty in communication or a question about your personality level." At this point, I think it would be appropriate for you to introduce yourself and to tell the other Soul the name of the personality level that you want to communicate about. Souls have more than one personality in physicality in the Now, so you have to be specific.

Now, speaking from your Soul level energies that surround you, explain to the other Soul the difficulty you are experiencing and the questions that you have. Remember, if you have difficulty with this, you can say right in your mind, "Soul, help me to speak my truth clearly and from the *highest level." You will receive help with your expression. It's just channelling. You Soul is going to start putting out more of those sounds and vibration to the other Soul, but this time it would be very helpful to provide some words so that you understand what is being said. You know for the most part what your Soul is going to say because you have already told your Soul what it was that was bothering you. Besides, your Soul knows already. You communicate well with it. Channel the words for your Soul, as your Soul tells the whole story to the other person's Soul and tells them what you want to know or what changes you would like to have.*

In this communication, try to be very specific about the circumstances of your issues and concerns with the other person. If this person is not well connected with their Soul, their Soul knows what they are doing much the way you see things through a pair of binoculars with a long distance view. It is not the same as being down there looking through the personality's eyes the way your Soul can do. Your Soul doesn't really need anyone to tell it what you are doing and feeling. However this other person may not have this quality of communication with their higher level. You might want to explain what the personality is doing and how it is affecting you, because you are in a very good position to describe the way things seem to be at the personality inter-action level. Remember not to allow yourself to slip down to the personality level at this time.

See now that the other Soul is speaking to you, trying to explain from its point of view what has been happening and the difficulties that the personality is experiencing. This is a channelling exercise. This Soul has been sending energy pulses to you, but you have learned how to turn them into words. Remember, it is not critical that your understanding is complete and perfect the first time you make this contact.

You can do this exercise many times if you want to with the same person. Don't get too serious or anxious about this. Use some words that simply feel right.

If you are having difficulty receiving the communication of the other Soul, use your imagination to assist you. Imagine that you can see the other person's face as you know it superimposed over the field of Light that is their Soul. It can be quite expressive if you use your imagination. What is that face and mouth seeming to say? This is a channelling exercise but it's very easy. As you gain a little bit of understanding of the other Soul's perspective, you may have a request. Did you know you can make a request? You can ask the other person's Soul to help you to arrange your relationship or communication with their personality level in a different way. If that person is fairly well connected with their Soul, the Soul will be able to have a direct effect. If not, the Soul will tell you and will be able to give you a suggestion as to how to deal with the person yourself in the most productive way for you. Go ahead and make your request.

After you have finished making your request, you might ask the Soul of the other person if there is something you can do for that Soul. Is there a certain thing that they would like you to say or do to assist them in helping their personality level evolve? Is there a message? I have found that it is a very fine and satisfying thing to be able to both give and receive in these communications. Complete your communication. If you do not feel that you have finished, perhaps you would like to make an appointment to go back and talk to this other one's Soul again. In some cases, I think you will find that you will need to have a number of conversations as you begin to understand each other better and as you begin to understand yourself more fully as you function in this particular relationship.

I would, at this time, suggest that you ask yourself, "What has been my share of the responsibility for the communication difficulty?" It would also be appropriate to ask your Soul what you should consider doing about your share of this responsibility. If you have called a Spiritual Teacher to you, you might want to ask for their input. Before the other person's Soul leaves, you might ask your Teacher to shed a little further Light on any matter that needs clarification. It is always useful to get someone else's perspective.

When you are complete with this process, bid goodbye to the other person's Soul. Remember to include an expression of gratitude for its service to you. I think that your Soul would certainly want to say a very loving goodbye and perhaps the two Souls will embrace. It would be very fine if you would participate in this loving farewell and allow the true respect and love that goes from Soul to Soul to be part of your experience. If you do, I think that you will truly understand what Soul level relationship feels like. After you have made your farewell, I think it would be appropriate to thank the Spiritual Teacher and your Soul for the assistance that they have given you in this process.

Then you and your Soul will begin to return down the corridor to the heart centre. If you feel in this exercise that you want further input from your Spiritual Teacher, just invite them back with you. See now that you enter into the heart centre and you sit down somewhere comfortably with your Soul and your Teacher, if you have invited one. At this time, it is very appropriate to discuss and review what has occurred. Perhaps there will be a realization, not just about your communication with this other person, but something about yourself and perhaps about communication upon the Earth plane. Try to formulate in words and concepts these realizations and to discover the practical applications you can make to your daily life and communications.

When you have completed this, feel yourself beginning to relax and to reoccupy your physical body. Feel yourself as very centered in the heart but also feel your consciousness expanding out and filling the whole physical body from the top of your head to the tip of your toes. Feel yourself becoming fully present in physicality again. As you do this, begin to release any extra channelled energy that you have within your structure. Release it right down to the bottom of your feet, beginning at the top of your head and letting it flow away like water down through the whole body and out into the Earth by means of the root chakra, the legs and feet. Feel it sliding away like beautiful golden water, and feel it flowing right down into the heart of the Earth. Allow your physical body to release any points of energy that might feel a little cramped or stuck.

Remember, you are in your column of Light and you are connected to the heart of the Earth. The realizations, the love and the sharing at Soul level that you still have within you will flow into the Earth and, through her, to humanity as a whole. Thus the power of your realizations and growth will enrich and nourish others as well. Feel, as always, the Earth's warm and loving response to you, thanking you for your Light and sending beautiful emerald green/gold energies spiralling up your column of Light, into your feet, moving up your body, softening, nurturing and nourishing you. This is communication of a very high order, that you and the Earth are sharing. You are helping to evolve each other as you communicate in this way. See now that the green/gold energy of the Earth moves up through your body out of the top of your head and up the column of Light. It touches right into the white Light of the Source level. The white and the green/gold energy blend together. See how mother Earth and the Source communicate through you, evolve through you.

This is the most wondrous relationship of all. You are the channel, the facilitator of this wonderful communication and we all honour you and thank you. As you are evolving yourself, the Earth and humanity and yes, even the Source, grow as well. This is a wonderful result of communications at a high level, isn't it? You are doing so well. See if you can make this work moment to moment in your daily life. You will be surprised. People will begin to respond to you in ways that you desire, not in ways that confuse or hurt you. Bringing the Soul level into your daily life in this way will make a lot of difference to the quality of your life. I, Vywamus, assure you this is so.

EVOLUTIONARY EXERCISES for CHANNELS

CHAPTER 3

Understanding The Four Bodies

I n this chapter we are going to discuss the four bodies and I will give you exercises to assist you in balancing and communicating with them.

In the previous chapter, we discussed communication and how communication and relationships are involved in your evolution in a very direct way. This truly is one of the main thrusts at this time of the Plan of our Source. As I view it, the Source, in order to evolve itself, differentiated Itself into distinct focuses that were able to communicate and form relationships, evolving each other and, thereby, the Whole.

To me, this means that you can use communication for almost everything. That is really what we are going to do with the four bodies. We are going to use a communicative patterning this time to balance and align them. Now there are other ways to balance and align the four bodies. You can visualize your four bodies in your inner vision and you can get them to line up in a nice even way, each of them having their heart centre centred on the etheric heart centre. This is a very helpful Light exercise, but we really want to go into a deeper level of balancing. I suggest that the communicative approach is very good.

The first point I would like to make is that, in a larger sense, you really have one, whole structure. However, for the purpose of studying and understanding this structure, I believe it is very useful to take it apart notionally. I generally speak in terms of your structure as being comprised of four distinct bodies, but I ask you to keep in mind always that it is more accurate to think of them as four aspects of one complete system which you are utilizing to remain present in physicality. Now let us pause and discuss for a moment why you do appear to have four of these structural aspects or bodies. Well, for one thing, the reason that you have four such bodies is so that you can live comfortably and effectively here on this planet.

This is a powerfully and intensely physical planet and that means that you have to have an energetic structure that is capable of anchoring you into the deep levels of the planetary electromagnetic field. We could refer to the body or capacity that enables you to do this as the "physical body". One of the things that I would like to say about the physical body, and I think this is a good point, is that it is not quite what you think of as your physical body. When I talk about your physical body you may make reference to the flesh and muscle and bone, but the part that I really see when I look at you is something that is what you would call the "etheric structure proper."

I am careful when I use that word "etheric" because when people talk about etheric body work, frequently they are talking about all of the aura, all the other bodies of your structure that are generally not so visible to the physical eye. When I talk about the "etheric body", I really mean the Light structure that underlies the physical flesh and bones. It is composed of the lines of force and the major and minor chakras, as I have said.

This wonderful energetic structure has the ability to create for you your own presence or space to occupy in this world. It permits you to have an electromagnetic field which vibrates at your own unique frequency and is capable of interfacing with and integrating you into the larger fields of the physical planetary consciousness. Without your etheric physical body, you would not be able to hold yourself present in matter on the planet. Because this body or aspect of you operates at the deep levels of material manifestation, some people have said that it operates in the third dimension. I think that this can be a helpful way to talk about it if you do not fall into the mistake of regarding this marvellous body as being lower or less evolved than the other three. We tend at times of late to refer to the third dimension in an almost negative or pejorative fashion and I do consider this to be a most unhelpful distortion of your reality.

You also have an emotional capacity. You have feelings. In fact, I think that you have noticed that the more you evolve, the more clear, strong, supportive and enlivening is your emotional life. This is very important to you as well. The emotional structure has an affinity with the flow of the life force within this world and is able to understand and respond well to it. Some people have spoken of this capability of the emotional body as being able to operate in the fourth dimension. I agree that this can be a useful way of looking at it. I regard the emotional body as the aspect of self which permits you to experience in an intense and immediate way the physical sensation of your own thoughts. I believe that emotion is merely thought experienced as a tangible flow. This ability you humans have to be in emotion is a function again of the mirroring, magnifying quality of physicality on this planet. To feel emotionally the sensation of your own responses to your thought processes is to live these thoughts, to be immersed in them and, ultimately, to know them intimately. What an incredible evolutionary tool emotion truly is! It is, of course, that aspect of you that we have sometimes called the emotional body that enables you to use this ability.

As well, you are enjoying very much having a mental life here. The mental qualities are really those that have to do with perceiving the structures of things, the designs and formations that underlie everything, like the skeletal structure that supports the body. When you go to a museum and you see the various skeletal structures of beings or animals that have been on the Earth but are no longer here any more, you only have to look at their structures and you get a very good idea of what they were like. Your mental body tunes into and is aware of structures, both potential and actual.

Now it has been said that your mental body has an affinity for the fifth dimension. This also can be a helpful way of talking about the role of the mental self in your life. You could say that its nature is really aligned with the dimension or energetic of conceptual form and structure. By this, I mean the underlying creative ideas of things as the Creator envisions them. In this modality or dimension you are connecting with the structure that supports everything in physicality. It also connects you through the higher conceptual levels into the essential order or blueprints of all Creation. It is the mental body then that enables you to innately grasp the ideal formats of things even though they may at first seem obscured from your vision. You notice that you all do have a sense when you look at things whether they are balanced and symmetrical or whether they appear to be distorted, lopsided or somehow not structured in a way that looks as though it would work well. Through your mental level you have a sense then of the ideal patterning. This is the general purpose for which you have a mental body.

Here upon the Earth plane another level of awareness has been developing for some time. You have been very involved in helping humanity to evolve to the point where they can use their fourth body effectively. This is the spiritual body. The spiritual body is a very embracing energy. When I look at it, I tend to see that your spiritual body seems to surround everything else that is part of your structure. It brings a point of beginning to a point of completion for you here on the physical plane. The spiritual body also interpenetrates all the other bodies. It has a kind of embracing or completing energy that helps you to feel that you are whole. In this physical world, it is the spiritual body which, in the earlier stages of your evolution, truly anchors the Soul's energy into your structure and provides a bridge for it to connect with the personality ego. As you progress in your development as a divine being in the physical world, this Soul bridge becomes broader and more comprehensive until the Soul consciousness interpenetrates and merges with all aspects of the Earthly self. It is the spiritual body which facilitates this process. Sometimes it is said that the spiritual body operates in a sixth dimensional or "essential" modality.

As I have already said, these four bodies are in fact a way of talking about one physical design structure which is completely whole and fully integrated. For this reason, you will almost never discover a problem with one body or aspect of yourself which is not also present in one form or another in all the other bodies. Each body or aspect of you is expressing in its own unique fashion something about you as a being, something that is significant for you to see and understand in the course of your evolutionary journey. This is one of the reasons why the physical world is so helpful to you in your progression to full self-realization. It magnifies and mirrors to you in a very concrete and tangible way the truths about your own state of being which you might find too subtle to comprehend in a less intense energetic environment. A healer who understands this will certainly be working on all the bodies to bring the whole of your structure into harmony and balance. Your journey in physicality involves evolving, developing, expanding and balancing those four aspects with your manifested presence.

What this discussion about your four bodies really means is that you are present and experiencing your physical existence simultaneously from the perspectives of all of these aspects of the self and you are doing it in an essentially integrated manner moment to moment in your life. When we want to talk about balancing your four bodies, one of the things we do is to give you an understanding that chronic imbalances in your energy structure most often come from you giving more focus, more importance, more direction, more energy to one body in preference to the others. This puts you out of balance because you are not fully present in the other bodies. You know of some people who seem to be extremely mental but they also seem to be very scattered physically. Sometimes they appear rather emotionally not there either, rather vague, and you don't feel a lot of depth and sincerity in their emotional level. Well, that has a great deal to do with the fact that they are not balanced. Balancing really isn't that difficult when you understand it more clearly.

Let us use an example to illustrate it. Let us say you have a gallon of energy and you have these four bodies or containers to put it in. It seems to me that you should ideally have one quart in each of the four focuses, unless you were engaged in a particular activity or even a particular life such that you deliberately set up an energy imbalance for an important reason. Some of the work that you have to do requires you to exert a lot of effort from one of your focuses temporarily. You have had experiences in which you have had to do something very, very difficult, say physically, perhaps to keep going beyond your point of natural comfort. What you have done is to draw energy out of the emotional, out of the mental and perhaps out of the spiritual focuses. You brought everything into the physical for that last burst of effort. That is why sometimes when you are making these tremendous physical efforts, you feel like you have a narrow, tunnel-like awareness, as if the whole of you is suddenly present in the physical body, giving you the last possible drop of energy that you have. Now that is an example of a useful imbalance if you had to complete that physical task and it was important. Sometimes when you are studying or reading something that is very, very important to you, you will find that you draw a lot of energy out of the physical, the emotional and even out of the spiritual focuses in order to do this very conceptual work. When you finish, you sometimes feel peculiar, as though you have been in a little box and you haven't seen the outside world for some time. Perhaps the physical body is very stiff and feels as though it has been sleeping and your emotional life feels like it has been narrowed to a little, tiny focus. This happens because you are out of balance, but you did this for a reason and as long as you understand that, you can then rebalance yourself by allowing that whole gallon of energy to be redistributed in a more even way. This has been a bit of an oversimplification but it illustrates the point quite well, I think.

The other thing that is so useful about my gallon of energy example is that it flows. Did you notice that? When you have four levels to put a gallon of energy in, you are going to see that the energy is a little like water in that it is going to move around right through all the four bodies. There isn't a particular energy in the gallon that says you can only use it in the physical, or that you can only use it in the mental. It is just a gallon of wonderful, cosmic energy and it flows throughout all of the bodies. Now that's one of the reasons you get out of balance fairly easily, because you can really put this energy anywhere you wish. It requires a knowing, conscious commitment to balance to use energy in all of the four bodies in a balanced, even way. You don't have something called mental energy or something called physical energy or something called spiritual energy or emotional energy. Many people think that. They say, "Well I am a high energy person physically, but I must say that mentally you know I haven't got it." Isn't that interesting? It really tells you about the commitment they have made for the use of their energy. Somebody else may say, "Well you know I am not physically strong but I am very, very clever intellectually." Again, it's a commitment to use their own life force in a particular unbalanced manner.

Another interesting thing is that you are not really limited to a gallon. You can always just say, "Please may I have some more." Many people who work on the spiritual level do ask for more energy. They connect with the Soul level and draw that energy in, but sometimes they think that this is only spiritual plane energy and that they can't use it in any other way or in any other body. They don't realize that it is just the same energy from the Source and that they could bring it in for the use of their other bodies quite nicely. In many cases, I think that they should really do that, because many people who have spent a lot of time looking at spiritual matters, when I view them, have large functioning spiritual bodies, but their structure thins down very quickly from there. I am really looking at the intensity and the effective use of energy. When we look at it this way, balancing isn't that difficult at all. It is really a question of taking a look at your life choices and also at your belief that perhaps you really only have a limited amount of energy available. You can ask your Soul for as much energy as you need, so you don't have to worry about dividing your limited amount up so anxiously. As well, it is time to realize that balance is just a question of how important you think each of your focuses or bodies are in a relative sense. Are you utilizing your energies from the perspective of equality?

It is time to start thinking of yourself not as a physical person or an emotional person or a mental person or a spiritual person. It is time to take more responsibility than that. You know some people just say, "That is the way I am. There is not much I can do about it. I am just a certain type of person." The truth of the matter is that you really have mastery over where you put your energy, particularly when you get to the evolutionary level at which you have four good structural aspects that are ready to serve you if you will allow them. It is a responsibility issue from my perspective and I sometimes laugh just a little when people come to me and say, "You know, Vywamus, I am such a mental person. I just really am not comfortable with all this emotional clearing that you like to talk about. I really feel that it is not my path." Well, I have to chuckle, because I can see that they do have four bodies alright. I can see that the mental might be rather inflated but this is just a matter of their decision making. If you take responsibility for your four body structure and responsibility for your connectedness into the Source level, then you can have all the energy you need and you can deploy it in a balanced way.

In my view, this brings us to the area of self-love. I would like to tell you that one of the reasons you don't give a particular body much attention or energy is because sometimes you don't feel as comfortable or as loving with its nature. Sometimes, it is like having four children and three of them are very difficult for you to relate to but you have one that seems just right to you. You really approve of this one. It is very hard for you not to give more of your attention and more of your affection to the one that really fits your idea of the way it should be.

In a lot of ways the personality ego is like that parent. Sometimes it feels, "Oh well, I like that mental one. He does everything properly. He never causes a fuss, screams or yells and every time I ask him to do something he just goes and does it; but that naughty little emotional one is always throwing fits and I just have a really hard time relating to it." Perhaps it is like a very physically focused parent who has four quite interesting children, one of which is very physically oriented while the others are not. You know very well that the parent is going to have a hard time giving equally to the other three. The parent unintentionally may give a lot of secret attention to the one that they can understand and feel comfortable with. It is a matter of self-love. If when you begin to connect with all of your bodies and you see that one is quiet and tired and has no voice at all, it is not usually because it is being uncooperative with you. It is more often because you have not given it much value. You have not loved it very much. Perhaps you have not appreciated what it can do, and so that is why it appears to you as rather frail.

The matter of being balanced is truly a responsibility issue. Sometimes when I say these things, people groan and say, "Oh no, not more responsibility." It is true that very often when I talk to you I tell you that you are responsible for this or responsible for that, but think about it. It means more freedom. It means that you don't have to be a certain kind of unbalanced person just because that's the way it is and you can't do anything about it. It is very easy when you begin to understand that it is really only a question of your decision as to how to allocate your particular resources.

Sometimes it is not always easy to tell how and when you may have made decisions or judgements which resulted in these preferences for one body, one focus, over the others that are part of you. Quite frequently, past life experiences are causal here. For example, perhaps you had a life in which you were very mental and you found that at some point your emotional focus began to surface but that it was perhaps a bit repressed and even a little angry for being sat on for so long. It came forth in a very explosive way and shattered what you thought of as your calm and rational life. You might at that time have made some very serious judgements against the emotional aspect of Self which would then have been piled on top of the ones you must already been holding to have such an imbalanced life in the first place.

Some people, as they travel along their evolutionary paths, make judgements against the way they used to be or they look at a particular faculty such as the emotional body and, because they have only seen its unhappy and repressed states of being, judge against the whole of it without trying to find out what it does when it is in a healthy condition. It is liberating to understand that the Source has carefully designed these wonderful four bodies and that they are all intended to support you where you actually are now in your evolution, where you have been in the past and where you will be in your next physical expression on the planet. It is important to remember that each is a part of a fully integrated, intelligent whole and that your physical totality can only operate at its optimum capacity if each body is allowed to function according to its true nature, without repression, without judgement. Our next step is to get to know what all the bodies do, so that you don't make judgements against them through lack of understanding about their role in your life and evolution.

Perhaps you think that you know what the physical body does, but I would like to tell you that you only know part of it. You know that it provides you with the ability to stay present in a body on the physical plane. You are quite aware of that and you are aware that in order to do this you have to eat and sleep and so forth, but you probably don't know that your physical body really is the means whereby you create on this planet. You see, the Earth is, as I have said, a very intensely physical consciousness and even when she takes her next evolutionary step, I believe that she will maintain this rich and vibrant focus. When you ascend from physicality you will not just do as some people when they graduate from university and take all their books and notes and throw them in a bonfire and say, "Well now I can forget everything." When you ascend, you will not do that. You will keep all your true knowledge and understanding gained while in physicality. After all, how do you suppose the Spiritual Teachers are able to incarnate to help out at a particular time? This would not really be available to them if they had forgotten all of what they had learned about how to utilize physical forms. They keep that quality within themselves that allows them to manifest a physical body that can integrate into a planetary structure. You don't really throw it out at all.

On this planet you have a very dense or, as I prefer to term it, a very intense, physical energetic field or body. Some have called this a "third dimensional" body. In the last few years, I have been steering away from speaking of dimensions as though they were separate zones of awareness. That is not quite the way it truly is on this planet, and so I like to emphasize a more whole perspective which focuses upon the variety of ways in which you are able to experience your own presence in this wondrous world. If you aren't truly present in your physical body you are not able to work and create fully in physicality. The creative plans and ideas that you have been working on may just stay in the spiritual, mental or emotional mode and never precipitate into the denser world of matter which is visible and tangible to the sense faculties which you are most experienced in using. You have had many experiences wherein your hopes and ideas seemed as if they were just about actualized. They were so real, so clear, so right and then they didn't happen. Sometimes you look back and say, "Well it was just as well", but sometimes you feel that some great event just touched you and missed. You know about your physical structure, the etheric body proper that I have been talking about. That's the one that brings your creativity through to your daily life. You could say that your first and second chakras, the root and polarity chakras, these are the ones that get together and bring into physicality the energy that you have brought in from the higher levels, your inspiration, your idea, your desire that it be so. This really comes into the second chakra area.

Now what I am giving you is more a model of the way the second chakra works on an ideal level. The higher vibrational energy comes in to the second chakra area and then, through the root chakra which is really the base of the physical structure, a lot of energy from the planetary structure comes in. It comes into the second chakra and it mixes there. You then have a blending of the higher energies, your inspiration and your passion to create, with the material, the energy of the Earth plane. It is there within the second chakra, that the energy of invocation truly comes into the physical world. It is not that you are creating only "from the second chakra", because you are bringing in all the higher energies, but somewhere they have to connect with the planetary energies, don't you think so? Most people think they connect way out in the void somewhere. They believe that they bring in their inspiration and then send it out somewhere and that mysteriously, where they no longer have control over it, it connects with the physical and then something happens.

Well that's not quite the way I view it. When you think about our models of creativity and how we have talked about them, it really doesn't make much sense that your creating would really be sparked somewhere beyond your area of mastery, does it? Then you would not have complete responsibility over the process, would you? There would be something going on out there that you had no control over and you could hardly say that you were a master of the process. It makes good sense when you think of it that the point of sparking or igniting the creativity that you have brought into the planetary structure must occur somewhere within you. Think about it. Where would be a good place? Somewhere where you are going to be able to draw in the energy from the planet, and somewhere where you are going to bring in all the inspiration from the higher Self. You might say the heart centre. That is true. Eventually, the energy that is blended in the second chakra comes up into the heart area.

Much of what is expressed actually comes forth from the throat centre. That is why we call it the second centre of creativity, the centre of expression. In the second chakra area you are blending energies which are drawn up to the heart where balancing, harmonizing and what you might call "fine-tuning" occurs. Then the energy comes up into the expressive centre. At the same time, certain other energies continue to flow in, coming down from the Soul Star and the mental centres within the head, but truly, the going forth area is the throat. Now isn't that interesting, because that is where you speak from. You know how important sound is. We actually do a lot with sound. Sometimes when an English-speaking channel is working with people whose first language is not English, there is still something in the sound that comes from the throat that has effect for the listener, even though the words themselves are not understood.

This is really a model, a general outline and there are many details that we could add as to how creativity occurs on the planetary level. If you are not using your physical body to help you with this, truly you are not going to make the final mixing, that final blending that creates something that is substantial in the world where your reality framework is anchored. So you really need to work with the physical body.

Let us now consider the purposes of the emotional body. It is a very magical body and it really has so many talents. This is why it is such a sorry thing to see someone who has shut down their emotional body. The emotional body has an affinity for the magnetic functions. It is not so much that it is, in its true nature, solely magnetic because it should, in fact, be a fully balanced electromagnetic system, but the manner in which the emotional body functions utilizes the principles of attraction and affinity to a very refined degree. That means it is capable of drawing things to it. As well, it connects. It is a connector that allows you to draw in and hold connections with other people and events of consciousness. It invokes and draws them to you. You know of people about whom you might say, "They don't feel real to me." Now you are not saying that they are imaginary. What you are saying is that you cannot feel anything from them. There is nothing really that connects with you, that gives you the sensation of their beingness. One of the things that you are noticing is that their emotional body is rather shut down, because it does not have that connective quality that allows you to interact with their energy. Remember what we have said about relationships. They are really communications or the sharing of energy. It is in the emotional body that this ability to interact intimately with another person is actually held. It is focused there. It is not that your other bodies don't connect up because, as I have said, you really communicate from all levels with another person, but let us say that the nuts and bolts of this capability are centred in the emotional body. It is the emotional body's evolution that the other aspects of self draw upon for their communicative abilities. So when you shut down the emotional body, this ability to be connected into another being is greatly impaired. The communicative functions of the other aspects of you do not really have much in the way of intensity in their interactions with others.

In the creative process, the emotional body does something ←
else. It is somewhat difficult for me to express what that is in your words. I think the statement, "Does it feel real?" expresses what I am trying to say. As an example of this, think of listening to a friend tell you about a theory that they have just discovered. They explain it, "I have just made a new break through. I believe this is the way such and such is." You listen and you say, "Well now, isn't that interesting." It has no burning quality of conviction for you and it does not

feel like your truth. However, if you should ignite with it so that you deeply and intensely feel the truth of it, it becomes a part of your understanding. There is an event that occurs in which you become connected with this idea on an emotional level and then you have the experience that it feels right to you. Saying "That feels right" is quite a lot different than saying, "That sounds sensible." It is a very different quality of experience. You can have something that sounds very sensible and rational that feels right too. When you have that deep, almost gut-level feeling that something is so and it also hangs together very nicely in the conceptual area, you know how hard it is for someone to talk you out of it. It is becoming your truth quite rapidly. It is "real" for you.

Another thing that this means is that if your emotional body is shut down, nothing feels very real to you. You have the feeling, and most people go through it now and again, that everything seems vague. People talk about a lack of commitment. They get quite disturbed about that sense that they are just floating along and nothing has any reality. That is an emotional situation because feeling, the intensity that comes to you from the emotional level, is what makes everything quite convincing and solid. When you are creating, it is the emotional body that helps you use energy in a special way so that there is an intense and solid quality to what you create.

The emotional body is also a centre for holding onto things. Now that can be a little bit of a problem and I think that is one of the reasons why many people have been rather critical of the emotional body. It functions, as I have said, very much along the lines of the magnetic principles. As I view it, it is not your magnetic creative centre but it functions similarly. Now what this means is that if you want to hold onto something deeply, it is through the emotional capability that you can magnetize and hold it.

This works very nicely when you are in a beautiful state and you say, "I always want to remember this. I never want to forget it. I am going to hold it in my heart forever." You are calling upon that magnetic quality that the emotional body has to imprint this wonderful experience into your consciousness. You all have had the experience of wanting to remember a loved ones's face. You can call upon the emotional body to magnetize it and to hold it strongly within you.

Now there are also many other things that you may want to hold strongly. For example, your ideal sense of who you are, and perhaps some of the realizations that you have had in your meditations. You really want to magnetize them in the emotional level and hold them so that you don't have that experience of having a flash of illumination and then, when you go to look at it again, it is gone. When this happens, it is frequently because you didn't magnetize it. Another thing that the emotional body really helps to hold is your sense of being real yourself. You know sometimes people go through a stage where they don't feel terribly real. They feel, "Who am I anyway? I don't know." They haven't really magnetized or held deeply within themselves their feelings about who they are, their thoughts about who they are or their sense of their own reality as a being. One of the very most important things to magnetize, I think, is your sense of your own Divinity. Sometimes you feel very powerful and very bright and very much a Divine being, quite unlimited, and then it seems to slip away and all of a sudden you feel very small, unworthy and not particularly Divine. Some of the work we do involves magnetizing very deeply in your core that sense of who you are as a Divine being that is unlimited and is merely playing at discovering an adventure that is called physicality. Magnetizing very deeply your unlimitedness is the thing that gives you joy forever in physicality. You can never truly feel limited, unworthy, small and attacked as long as you have held deeply at the core of you this Divinity. So you see there is a great deal that is very wonderful to be said for this ability to hold and magnetize things.

Now, of course, one of the problems is that you magnetize all the unpleasant things too if you want to hold on to them. There are many experiences that you have had on the physical plane that you have magnetized very strongly. Death situations seem to spring to mind or situations in which you have been so unhappy that you have said, "I shall never forget this for the rest of my life. I shall never forgive. I shall never let this go." You magnetize when you say that and the experience and your responses to it at all levels come along with you for lives and lives. That is one of the things we have to do when we use a past life regression exercise. You go back and let go material that is magnetized to you but is no longer serving you. Isn't that interesting that we use the words, "let go." It does seem to be what you do when you are not wanting to magnetize or hold anything any longer. This is one of the main reasons why the emotional body has received such a bad reputation for many people. It is most often in the emotional body that you store the painful impact of these things. It is not necessarily the emotional body that has made the decision never to forgive and forget and yet it is the one that gets blamed for everything because that is where you put things. It is really the centre for holding and magnetizing. So you might want to take another look at some of the judgements that you have made against the emotional body and realize that, although it is sometimes hard to release things out of the emotional body, it is not because the emotional body chose on its own to store them in the first place.

Let us go back to our example of the children and you being the parent with a child that has a certain kind of quality that you perhaps invoked at one time. However, you do not particularly like that part of yourself that is responsible for this invocation, so you blame that child who has really come in with that quality because it has been drawn by your energy. Like attracts like, and sometimes you get very annoyed at a child of yours that is too much like you in a way that you have been unable to accept and embrace. That is the way you treat your emotional body at times. It is just following your basic lead in storing things that you have decided to store. Then, when you see what you are holding, you may get a sense of the state you must have been in to store things in the way you did. You get very disgusted and you sometimes reject the emotional body.

Yet the emotional body is really only holding a very small percentage of undesirable things. It is also keeping present for you all the glory of all the things that you have learned and seen in this wondrous Creation and your adventures through it. It has stored pictures of Divinity, pictures of other planets and planes and wondrous events at all levels.

You certainly have encountered points in the physical body where you have been storing things, but nevertheless, the central focus or headquarters for magnetizing really is the emotional body. So it is the emotional body that can help you a great deal in your processing if you ask it. It will surely tell you what you have stored and what, therefore, is still part of your consciousness that you are creating from, perhaps in a way that you do not like. Also, of course, the emotional body can assist you to magnetize all those glorious things that keep your sense of Divinity and connection to All That Is bright and fresh before you as you continue through your evolutionary journey.

Next, let us look at the mental. What do you suppose the mental body does? You already know a lot about what I like to call the everyday mental, which represents a lower vibrational level of the mental. That is not to say that we will throw it out as you expand. No, indeed you will retain all the wonderful things that the lower mental does, the analyzing, the logic and common sense and the conceptualizing. Surely you would want to retain these wonderful capabilities.

There is, however, a higher level of the mental body's function which we often call "knowingness". This is a kind of understanding that transcends knowledge and really goes into beingness. It is a place wherein a great deal of knowledge or information is worked through. This information comes from the physical body, from the emotional body, from the lower mental faculties, from the spiritual body, and yes, even from the Soul and other higher levels of consciousness. It is in the higher level of the mental body that you really blend all of those ways of knowing and you reach a state which is really a "beingness". You become that which you seek to know and understand and therefore your knowledge in that way is very multi-focused, very holistic and complete.

Now that sounds very wonderful. How do we get into that capability, that higher mental? Well, of course, it is an evolutionary process, but I like to say that the bridge really is the imagination. I think that it is the imagination that helps you move from that which is known and ordinary and truly a part of your way of looking at things to the unknown, to the new, to the exciting, to the unmapped and, for you, to your next step. For you, imagination is like an explorer or a pioneer. It goes forth into unmapped territory and lights it up, perhaps not in the careful, thorough and structured way that you think of as mental, but in a wonderful, inspirational fashion that allows you to see the path before you. Of course, as you travel that path, that which you pass through then becomes the known territory. You map it and you analyze it and you understand it. As you move forward with the imagination, the imagination really takes you into the higher levels of knowledge, into the higher ways of knowing things because it takes you to places you really haven't been before, wondrous places where everything is quite connected.

I always like to encourage everyone to use their imagination. People say to me, "Well, I really want to activate my third eye. How ever am I going to do that?" I suggest using the imagination. That is because what you understand as the third eye capability is really the higher knowingness that I have been talking about. It is not just a seeing at all. It is a complete understanding that transcends knowledge into beingness, and, as I have already suggested, the imagination is the path. So, when in our meditations I ask you to see this or that, please use the imagination like the pioneer, the explorer that is going out to map or open up a pathway to that which you do not yet know. We use the imagination to go into this new realm of understanding.

One of the things we sometimes notice when we are working with the mental body is that the mental body is really so delighted with what it can do, and you as Self are so delighted with what it can do, that you imagine that it really is the place that you are going to, the state of consciousness that you are seeking, and that all that has come before perhaps should be discarded. Well of course, we know that this is really not the way evolution works at all, Each level builds upon the previous level. You may discard that which is a distortion or that which is incomplete or inadequate, but you really do not discard that which forms a firm foundation for your next step. At times, when you deal with the four bodies, you may find that the mental sees itself as perhaps the zenith or the height of your evolution and is perhaps not as interested as some of the other bodies in cooperating and hearing from other points of view. You can help your mental body understand that it is really a very important and special focus, but that it is not the only one, that it is not the only point from which you experience your understanding and your growth. You evolve as the Source does in a complete way, from all the focuses that you are able to understand and view as Self.

Now let us consider the spiritual body. The spiritual body is a capability that you activate as your evolution through physicality advances, because the spiritual body has a wonderful ability to bring through from the higher levels, and particularly from the Soul level, the essence of Divine ideas. The potentiality that is the Light of Divine ideas comes through to you from the Soul level through this focus. The spiritual body has a way of reaching into the essence of things and of expressing them in their complete potentiality. Then they are brought into the mental where the structure begins to be put in place, and the creative process continues into physicality as essence becomes actualized through the support and work of all the bodies or focuses of Self.

The spiritual body does have another very important quality as well. It is very much there to remind you of the connectedness of All That Is. It has an embracing or completing quality and of course it is the outer-most layer, if you want to look at it that way, of your auric field. It embraces and interpenetrates and really gives a completeness to the whole of your structure. It is usually the first part of you that makes contact with the Soul level and it is very supportive of you as you move in your development towards complete connection with the Soul. I do not wish you to think that I am saying that the Spiritual body, because of its overview or its connectedness to the Soul level, is better or more advanced than the other three aspects or bodies. This is not so. The Spiritual body does indeed give you, if you let it, an expanded view of your cosmic reality framework, as you have been able to formulate it as a Soul at this point in your evolutionary journey. This does not mean that its vision is "perfect" or whole. It simply means that it is able to hold before you the fullest understanding that you have been able to achieve to date on a "spiritual" or comprehensive level. Many of you are coming to understand in these last few years that your ideas of what it is to be human and Earthly are very distorted and negative and do not truly give you a picture of the glory of your place within creation. These distortions have been held in the Spiritual body focus from the very earliest of your experiences on this planet. They have continuously been presented to you by the Spiritual body as intrinsic and key cosmic truths which have formed a substantial portion of the foundation of human mass consciousness from the beginning of time as you have known it on this planet. It is only now, as you begin to value and to listen to the input of your other body focuses, particularly the emotional and physical, that you are able to see through and let go of these ancient distortions of your reality. No one body focus is capable of grasping the Whole. You can only succeed in this when you operate from a fully integrated and balanced wholeness within yourself.

As we have already said, it is important that all of your bodies and the whole of Self come to understand the equality of these four focuses. They are unique. They have very special roles to play but none is more important than the other. Together they allow you to be all that you can be and anchor you very effectively into your experience of physicality, while keeping you connected with All That Is. Now of course that is the ideal arrangement that I have given you. That is what you have when you have full balance and alignment. "How do we keep things in balance?" you might ask. As I have said before, it is really only a matter of intention and truly it is something that is within your control. Eventually, you will reach the stage in your understanding and knowingness when you really feel and understand the equality of each one of the bodies and the special uniqueness of each focus. You will see that the Creator has designed your ideal structure so that all the bodies work together and support each other as each one works in its fully empowered form. That is the ideal. It is really not so very difficult for you once you have grasped the basic universal principal of the Divine equality of all things, all points of consciousness. The matter of balance comes with the understanding of this principle and with giving it loving effect within your life rather than playing favourites among the expressions of Self. I wish also at this time to remind you once again that the concept of a four body system is merely a tool, a way of talking about reality. It is not the reality itself. Do not become so wedded to the idea that you have a distinct four body structure that you cannot let this idea go as well when your greater Self calls upon you to do so. I believe that this will happen fairly soon in this fast moving life that you are now living, cosmically speaking. Use the tool we are providing in love and in wholeness and be prepared to lay it down gently when the appropriate time comes.

We have a little exercise we can do at this time to assist you in understanding and creating balance within your structure. It is a light and energy exercise that helps you to balance in a very immediate sort of way. It is a visualizing exercise and so I ask you to use your imagination.

CHANNELLING EXERCISE III
Balancing and Enlivening the Four Body Structures

In this exercise, we are going to draw some structures and we are going to use a pen but it is a Light pen. It draws lines of Light. We can get it to draw lines of Light in any colour we want.

Let us begin with the physical structure. Draw the physical structure in whatever colour of Light seems appropriate to you. We will start with a nice head centre. Perhaps you will draw something that is a bit like a skull, or a brain/mind sort of thing. It can be just round if you like. Then let us draw the spinal column and right at the bottom of the spinal column let's make a nice circle for the root chakra. Let us draw in the other chakras: the second chakra, the solar plexus chakra, a nice big heart centre chakra and then to the throat chakra, the third eye chakra and the crown chakra at the very top of the skull diagram. If you like you can add to that some lines that will indicate that we have some arms and legs here on this structure. I think it would be appropriate to put some smaller chakras in each of the hands and feet. Know of course that we have many other small lines and circles that we could add. Around all of this draw an outline now. Draw it all around these lines we have made in the shape of the human body. That is quite easy. What colour are you using for the physical? Something nice and bright that suggests the vibrancy of the life force as it pulses into the physical would be appropriate, I think.

All right now, you may stop drawing. Imagine that there are many coloured dots of Light. They are the same colour as the outline you have made. They are dancing throughout the whole of this structure you have drawn. See that the colour is very intense because there are many dots of Light. They are very close together and they are moving, because they are alive. Energy always has life, does it not? It is the Divine life force. Now let us fit that structure right over your physical body. See yourself manoeuvring that Light drawing that you have done inside your head and let's move it right over your physical body. Can you see it? Line up the chakras and everything until it fits quite nicely.

Now lets us draw the next body. It's going to be the emotional body. Let us pick an appropriate colour. It is a vibrant warm and flowing colour. Take up your Light pen again and this time draw a figure all around the one that you have already drawn for the physical. Draw this emotional body so that it extends two to three inches all around the physical one you have drawn. Draw the outline all around, under the feet and around the whole body, around the top of the head. Now, using our pen with the same colour we have used for outlining the emotional body, let us draw circles where all the chakras for the physical body are, but a little bit larger, so that they overlay the ones you have drawn for the physical, just a little bigger. Would you do that with your pen now? We can start with the crown chakra. Now draw in the third eye chakra, the throat and the heart chakras. Draw in the solar plexus chakra, the second chakra and the root chakra. Circle the ones in the hands and feet as well.

Put down your pen and see with your imagination that this emotional body structure is filled with more points of Light just as the physical was. These points are perhaps a little lighter in intensity of shade than the ones in the physical are and they are a little farther apart. They are moving and vibrating very nicely. Now see that they interpenetrate right into the physical structure you have chosen. They appear in the spaces between the dots that are part of the physical body. There is room for them but there are less of them that the dots of the physical body. Because the shade is just a little lighter in colour, you can really see that the physical body is perhaps the most dense and intense, much more solid. Now please ensure that this emotional body Light structure you have drawn fits well over the physical structure and is superimposed over your actual body as you sit and do this exercise.

Take up your Light pen again and let us make another drawing. This time it will be the mental body. What colour of Light will you choose to come from your pen? Pick a colour of Light that seems precise and clear as the mental body loves to be. Now begin to draw your outline. You will outline all around about three to five inches out from where the emotional body was drawn, all around, under the feet right around to the top of the head. You will see that it is *roughly human shaped but it is getting a little less so as you expand it. Now draw some more circles with the same colour of pen for the mental body all around the chakra centres. Start with the crown chakra. This time, it is even a little bigger that the circle drawn for the emotional body so it really goes all around it, but it is still centred from the same point in the centre of the circle, and the same with the third eye chakra, the heart chakra, the solar plexus chakra, the second chakra and the root chakra. See that we have a nice series of circles then and that they are coming out from the same centre points in three different colours. Encircle the chakras at the hands and feet as well.*

Now put down your pen of Light and see that there are dancing points of Light of the same colour for the mental body as the outline, but again, they are a little farther apart than the ones for the emotional body and they are perhaps a little less intense in shade. Now see these wonderful little points of moving Light that are all part of the mental body and how they are interpenetrating the emotional body, and yes, the physical body as well. Of course there aren't as many of them as there are in the emotional body and certainly there are a great many more in the physical body. You see that in the spaces between these other wonderful little points of Light those from the mental body can fit in quite nicely. See now what you have. Isn't that lovely? Very colourful, I would say.

Now let us get out our Light pen again and, using another colour, we will draw the spiritual body. For the spiritual body pick a lovely colour that really has an embracing, clear and high quality. It is a colour with a lot of Light and really very whole. Now begin with your Light pen and draw an outline. I would say that this one can be quite a bit farther out beyond the mental body. You might draw it out about 6 inches but in some people it gets out quite far, about 2 or 3 feet. Draw it wherever it seems appropriate to you. Draw it all around, under the feet, around the whole outline, right to the top of the head. See that it is surrounding the mental, emotional and physical structures quite nicely.

Using our Light pen again, let us encircle all the chakras starting with the crown chakra, making a little bigger circle than with the mental body in the same colour as that with which you outlined the spiritual body. Then encircle the third eye chakra, the throat chakra, the heart chakra, the solar plexus chakra, the second chakra and the root chakra. Again, all four of the circles at each chakra are radiating out from the same centre point in four different colours. These colours represent four different rates of vibration of energy. Encircle the chakras in the hands and feet as well. This is getting to be quite an interesting diagram of Light. See it all around you because you have drawn it that way. See that there are moving points of Light, little dots again of the same colour of Light in which you drew the outline of the spiritual body. They are moving too. Again, they are just a little less intense than the shade of colour that was used in the mental body. They are also farther apart than the mental body points of Light. See now that they interpenetrate the dots in the mental body, the emotional body and the physical body. They fit very nicely into the spaces that are left. Look at what we have now, a beautifully drawn, aligned diagram of your aura. Isn't it beautiful and intricate? We can see the different colours and vibrational rates of these intercon-nected parts of your structure.

Do you notice something else, my friend? The structure is really empty. There is no one home. We are waiting for someone to move into this wonderful structure. I think that it would be you. So now reference or draw with a wonderful white blue Light the Soul star which is right above the head of this diagram, at least three or four inches higher up from the top of the spiritual body. Draw it with a nice white blue Light, very clear and intense. Now we are going to occupy from the Soul level this wonderful auric structure that we have created, this four body system. To me, the structure itself looks very nicely aligned and balanced and everything is ready and waiting.

From the Soul star with your pen of Light you are going to draw three lines of lovely blue white Light. They are really going to flow down from the Soul star. The first one is going to go into the middle of the head, right into the radiant third eye centre point. The next line flows directly to the heart centre. I would say we will pinpoint that centre point from which all the heart chakra circles radiate. Anchor it nicely in there. Then we are going to put a third line right down into the central point from which the root chakra circles emanate. Now we have three good solid lines of life force energy coming down from the Soul level.

Now let's activate our structures. You could see a switch on the wall that says "On". Pull it now and see energy begin to pump into the structures from the three lines of force, pumping Light in a very unlimited way from the Soul level. Fill up all the bodies until everything is well lit with this wonderful blue white Light. Feel how this Light is all around you now. We have drawn this structure all around you, so bring the Light into you. See all the Light pumping in from the Soul level. Look around. Are there any parts that perhaps have more of this Light than the others? Look again. I think you will see that perhaps one or two of the bodies will have more of this Light, and one or two don't seem to be very well lit at all. That doesn't seem quite balanced, does it? Well, we know that we have an unlimited amount of energy to bring in from the Soul level. What we are going to do then is to pull in more energy from the Soul star. That's right - through those three lines of force. Draw it in strongly

64

with the force of your intention and of your love for Self.

Now we want to get some dynamic movement here. Let's get it moving. Let's move all the energy through the structures, quickly and flowingly, bringing it in around and around, through the physical, through the emotional, through the mental, through the spiritual, back into the physical, emotional, mental and spiritual, around and around and around, physical, emotional, mental spiritual, around and around and around. This energy is very dynamic. Use it to fill any parts of your structure that aren't bright.

See now that you have a glowing structure, full of Light. The Light is moving around and around. The energy isn't stuck at all. First it is in the spiritual and then it becomes mental and then it becomes emotional and then it becomes physical, around and around, flowing and moving in any direction that it wants. You see that the energy is all just one kind of energy, Source Light energy, life force energy. It is all the same. It is only the focus in which you happen to be utilizing it that makes any difference.

See that each body is just as intense and well lit as the others. You can see the currents of energy swirling from body to body, around and around with joy. No separation here, no boundaries, no barriers. You can move the energy from one to the other, back and forth, around and around, utilizing it fully in any way you want. See what a wondrous structure you have now, a fully bright and flowing auric field with all the bodies utilizing all the energy they need in a completely balanced manner. See how the chakras are lined up perfectly around those central points, vibrating and radiating. Look how the energy is swirling in all those chakra circles you have drawn, pumping energy through and swirling around and around to the crown chakra, the third eye chakra, the throat chakra, the heart chakra, the solar plexus chakra, the second chakra, the root chakra, the hand chakras and the feet chakras. See the large, circling chakras of force and Light moving around, distributing the energy, filling and energizing the whole structure.

Now my friends, you feel very balanced I would say, and you look very balanced from here. I think you will find that this exercise will aid you greatly. I would suggest that you use it as often as you wish. More and more you will feel that you are a whole being with a number of different points of view, rather than a fractured collection of separated aspects.

CHANNELLING EXERCISE IV
Balancing the Four Body Structure Through Communication

I would like to give you another exercise for balancing the four bodies, but this is more a communicative one. Remember that I have said that communication is the patterning that the Source is using to evolve. I have also said that communication is really a sharing of energy. This is a channelling exercise, and I will ask you to reference your column of golden Light which is actually there all the time now, isn't it? See how it is anchored firmly in the centre of the Earth, and that it extends beautifully and powerfully right up to the Source level, complete, unbroken, powerful and so bright that it fills you will wondrous Light and clarity. You feel very secure in this column of Light.

Enter into your heart centre in the way you have always done. Once again, using your imagination, see this wonderful heart centre as a place and see that there is a big beautiful table of the kind that we have at very important meetings. There are quite a number of comfortable looking chairs all around the table. You, the conscious self, the personality level, you are sitting at the head of the table. Look at the other end of the table. There is your Soul, looking very pleased and delighted. Yes, this table is really a symbol of, well, you could call it "The Governing of Self" where the moment to moment important decisions for Self's evolution are made. The conscious self, and, because of your evolution and your commitment, the Soul, are now a part of these decisions making moments.

Listen. Let yourself hear that there is a knock at the door which is at the other end of the room. Go to the door and open it. Who is there? It is the physical body consciousness. Using your imagination give the physical body a wonderful colour, perhaps several of them. Let them be colours that really suggest the solid supportiveness of the physical body, its strength, its competence and the wondrous contribution it makes in helping you to integrate comfortably, safely and in health into this magnificent Earth plane. This colour should also reflect the service that it is doing, offering a structure through which the Soul can anchor here upon the Earth as part of its evolution and its service. Give it a face or features that show its qualities. Show the physical body its place at the table. Give it a chair and really make it feel welcome. Give it love and acceptance and let it know how happy you are that it has come.

Now there is another knock at the door. You call, "Welcome, come in." Look, it is the emotional body consciousness and it has come to join you. Give it a colour or colours that reflect its wonderful flowing, flexible energy. Let the colours show forth its connective, communicative qualities and its ability to magnetize to you all that is bright, beautiful and wondrous and hold it there in strength and stability. It is a wonderful body which helps you to feel very real indeed. Give it perhaps a face, and an appearance that shows your understanding of how it supports you and how it is supporting the Soul in its connective activities. Show the emotional body its seat and make it feel very welcome. Give it love and acceptance and let it know how glad that you are that it is here to be a part of the decision making of Self.

There is another knock at the door. You call, "Welcome, come in." Look, it is the mental body consciousness. Give the mental body a colour or several colours and an appearance that suggest its clarity, its precision, its vision and its conceptual power. It is very supportive and connecting in its own way. It is the one that envisions the structures that everything you create is built upon, like the bones of your body or the inner structures of buildings. The mental body provides the strength and support mechanisms upon which everything else rests. Show your understanding of this in the colours and appearance that you give the mental body and guide it to its place here at the table. Give it welcome and help it to understand how glad you are that it is here. Give it love and acceptance now.

There is yet another knock at the door. "Welcome! Come in," you call. It is the spiritual body consciousness. Give the spiritual body a colour or colours and appearance that shows forth your understanding of its wondrous ability to bring through to you the essence of your highest understanding of the Creator's ideas. It has a connective quality that is very embracing. It shows you the wholeness of things and the potentiality of the ideal patterns that come in from the Soul level. Acknowledge the way it is supporting your growth here on the Earth, helping you to connect with the higher ideals as a doorway through which the Soul can come into physicality. Show it its place at the table and give it welcome and acceptance and love.

Now that all four bodies are present, I think that it is important for you to stand up before them all and give them a good welcome. I suggest that you tell them that you regard them all as equals and that each one is essential in their wonderful unique specialities that add to the full functioning of Self. Please point out that none is better than the other, and that you would not be able to function to your ideal without any one of them. After you have made these statements it would be appropriate to tell them that when they come into this room they are free to speak their truth the way that they see it, and that they should never fear rejection or ridicule or any unpleasant response if they speak openly. Promise that you will support them and explain why it is so important that they communicate, each one in equality, for that truly is how you achieve balance. After you have done this, would you please introduce them to the Soul. Explain that it is your Soul and that the Soul is here to support each and every one of them and to help them achieve a balanced understanding of that which is the highest and best for Self and Self's evolution within the Plan of the Creator. Please do that now.

When you have finished, I think I should tell you now that at this point you can ask the bodies anything about their points of view on any subject. You will be able to process all kinds of interesting things by simply gathering them together and asking them what their opinions are on any issue, problem, relationship or person.

I think to begin with that we should ask them how they feel about the way Self has been evolving and growing and the way that you as conscious Self have been running the show. I think you will want to invite them to give their opinions and to talk about any problems, concerns or worries that they may have. It is important to show them that their truths count and are very, very important to you. This is how you will gain their trust, acceptance and willingness to participate in this process. Once they see that their views are accepted and welcomed and that there is no competition between them for your love and your attention, then you will find that they speak freely and honestly. It is not that they will not disagree at times. That sometimes happens, but they will find with the help of the Soul a truth that is true for them all.

Now it would be appropriate for you and Soul to stand up and go around the table to each body asking them how they feel about how you as conscious Self have been operating and if they have any suggestions, worries or concerns. You can begin with the physical body consciousness. Now you may find sometimes at first that some of these bodies do not want to talk very much. Perhaps they are shy because they have never been asked for their opinion before and have not been very involved. Perhaps they are afraid to speak because they have spoken their truth before and it has been rejected, ridiculed or denied. You may have to do a little coaxing at first and you know that the Soul would be very, very helpful with this.

Now remember, this is a channelling exercise and you are the channel and that means you will give the words to the bodies and to the Soul and to the conscious Self. Perhaps before you begin, you would like to invite one of the Spiritual Teachers to come with you. If you have a Spiritual Teacher that you would like to invite to become a part of this process you simply have to ask the Soul to invoke them to come or call them yourself. You will see that very quickly there will be a knocking at the door within your heart to the Spiritual Plane. If you go and open the door you will see that standing there is the Spiritual Teacher that you have called. Ask them to come in and give them a seat at the table. Whenever you need some help, clarity or better understanding with this process, call upon us and we will help. You will see.

As conscious Self, accompanied by the Soul and perhaps a Spiritual Teacher, go to each one of the bodies and talk with them. If a difficulty arises or if you do not know how to respond to the questions or comments of a body consciousness, then ask Soul and your Teacher to give you the words and the understanding to help this body to feel safe and able to participate and be part of the governing of Self, both in your daily life and in your life on the inner planes. Go around the table to each one and spend as much time as is necessary to assist each one to feel that they can speak freely and express their truth. I think that one of the things that you are going to find is that if you will provide the words through your channelling abilities, the Soul is going to make a commitment to each and every body to help and support each one equally and to promote the truth and under-standing of each one. I think you will also find that the Soul is going to make a commitment to listen to them and to assist in finding answers and solutions for their problems. It would be very excellent if you, as conscious Self, made a similar commitment to each body so that when they spoke within the heart centre, you would not ignore or deny any of them. You would give full acceptance to each for their truth. I think that this is what they are going to need to hear from you as conscious personality ego, dear ones. Indeed, I do.

When you have completed this stage in the process, let everyone go back to their seats. Then I think that Soul will probably want to stand up and make a statement of com-mitment to them all, and perhaps an expression of the joy that Soul feels in having everyone present to be a conscious part of the growth of Self. I think that you will also find that each time you do this exercise, the Soul will gather the truths that have been stated by each body and summarize them. The Soul will be able to blend all the energies of all the views expressed into a balanced whole which will contain and express the truths of all. From this wholeness perspective, each focus of your consciousness will be right and none will be "wrong". At the end of each one of these exercises, please channel for the Soul so that the Soul, with your assistance, is able to complete this important integrating and balancing function, which is, after all, one of the most important goals of the exercise. Perhaps the Spiritual Teacher that you have asked to participate will have something to add from their own knowledge and experience to the blended perspective achieved by all.

When you are finished with the exercise, come back into your physical body. Fully occupy it from your head to your toes with your consciousness and then, opening your feet, allow the channelled energy that is in your structure to gently flow out like water from the top of the head down into the Earth. Feel the Earth's loving response flow up from her core into your feet, filling your body with clear, nurturing green/gold energy. Feel that beauteous energy flow upwards in your channel of Light and touch, fully and lovingly, into the Source. Feel the joy of this connection and your part in it. Rest comfortably in this energy until you feel nurtured and strengthened.

CHAPTER 4
The Heart Focus

What I want to talk to you about in this chapter is a matter that is really very important. I think that it is one of the very most important things that I have ever talked to you about and that is the heart focus. You have heard the heart focus mentioned many times, I think. You have probably noticed that the exercises that I have given you for channelling all seem to centre on the heart. Perhaps you have asked yourself "Why is that?" It is time for us to talk about this.

From my perspective, the best place to begin is the Source, and the Source's Plan for evolving Itself. I think that I am being reasonably accurate when I say that the Source you identify with, which I will call "this" Source, chose to evolve itself through what we could describe as a diversification plan. It diversified itself into many, many conscious focuses, so that it could view experience from these many focuses and have a well rounded and whole picture as it grew and evolved. Now as I have already said before, we have a communicative patterning for the evolution of the Source and for you as part of the Source. That involves continuous energy exchange between different focuses, different points of consciousness.

Now you might have said to yourself at some point, "That's all very interesting. I see that there are many ways of looking at one particular experience, but what does that give you? Just a lot of different points of view, many of which don't really seem to fit together. That looks a little fragmented and confusing to me." You know, dear ones, if we left it just like that, that's exactly what it would be, confusing and maybe even a little fragmented. This is where the heart comes in. The heart focus is a very special kind of perspective that the Creator has understood to be the most important or key point in the development of the Plan for evolution of All That Is. It is in the heart centre and through the energies of the heart that all the different points of view and focuses are blended in order to bring forth one whole truth for beingness.

I think a very good way of looking at this is to picture a circle. There are an infinite number of points around it, but let's use twelve points and see that each of the twelve points are viewing the circle from a different vantage and certainly a different perspective. How are we going to blend all these perspectives into something that is whole? Well I think there is one more point. There is a point right in the middle that is the point I call beingness. This is the place in which you really become the whole of the experience. I think that comes very smoothly and naturally after you have gone around the circle and experienced a particular truth from all the different focuses. Then suddenly, there you are. You can stand in the centre and be the experience because you have experienced it from all points of view. This beingness is a blending. It is a bringing together of all the energies of the different points of view or focuses.

How is this blending done? It is through the heart focus. The Creator has planned it that way. Every point of consciousness within the great Creation of this Source has something that you could refer to as its heart centre or its heart focus. The energy that moves through that point of consciousness, perhaps it is a being like yourself, can be integrated and blended into a wholeness within the energy format that we call the heart focus. The heart is such an allowing and encompassing place that within its energy all points of view are right and none are wrong. They are all part of the truth. No focus is really better or more right than another because they are all perfectly right. They are all viewing reality, existence and experience perfectly well from their particular focus, so, of course, they are right. Even the focuses that seem to be very, very different and unique are all simultaneously right too.

In the heart, these differing points of view are really just aspects of a whole beingness. That is why the heart energy is so very loving. It is through the heart focus that the Creator expresses Its love for all that has been created, for all its points of consciousness. Divine love flows into the heart and from the heart out to others. As I have said before, the Divine Plan has many, many levels and within those levels, there are many, many points of consciousness, all relating and communicating. It is through that wondrous network that the energy of Divine love flows, through the heart centres of each and every point of consciousness.

It is also important to consider one of the other great gifts of this Creator. At a certain point in evolution, the experience of free will actualizes. It is a potential for all points of consciousness, and at a certain level of development it actualizes. It is possible to choose to live and to experience with your heart centre wide open so that all the love of the Source flows right through you and from you to other parts of the Divine Plan that you are communicating with. It makes for a wondrous support system. It is the true support system that the Creator arranged for within the Plan, intending that there would be many points of consciousness, all viewing experience from different focuses, and yet all connecting and communicating through their heart centres so that the love of Divinity would flow in an unlimited way throughout Creation.

I am sure that you can see how experience and evolution from this perspective would be a loving, joyous process of sharing Light and love. In that arrangement, no one would feel separate, isolated or unsupported. No one would be lost, because if their hearts were open they would always be connected with the Source through the Source's loving network of support. However, you know, you do have free will, and therefore, at a certain point you can choose to close your heart centre. You know what happens then. That is the very closest thing to experiencing complete isolation and separation. Now I say the "closest thing" because you know in reality that you are part of All That Is, and therefore you don't truly become completely isolated ever, although you are able to give yourself the illusion that you are. However, if you close your heart centre you can certainly have the experience of being isolated, of deciding not to rely or call upon the support system and, of course, of not receiving and giving love.

There are many wondrous qualities that make up this heart focus, qualities that you could say go into the energy mix that gives the heart the wonderful blending, uniting capacity that it has. There are heart qualities such as honesty, gratitude and, of course, unconditional love. There are allowingness, acceptance, joy, grace, and there are harmony, peace and security. Can you think of other qualities of the heart? I know you can if you pause and consider it. All of these qualities go together to make up an energy format that is capable of accepting and blending all points of view into a wonderful oneness that is really the experience of the Source Itself.

As you can see, when you choose to close down the heart you really are making a very important choice, aren't you, because you are saying, "I can do without all those qualities very nicely. I don't have to give or receive any of that." One of the things that sometimes happens is that you feel very left out and very isolated. You also find that your evolution sometimes slows down a bit because you are not really giving and receiving the wonderful energy that is moving throughout the whole of Creation all the time. Communicating, relating and sharing with each point of consciousness that you encounter aids the evolution of Self and of the whole. There is a lot you are saying "no" to when you decide to shut down your heart.

Opening the heart after it has been closed for a while feels a little difficult. Sometimes the heart is closed down because of false beliefs or impressions about reality. You see many people who say, "I do not want to have my heart open because others will just hurt me. I am very vulnerable there and they will come and hurt and attack me." So often when people are feeling insecure or fearful and separated from their own power as Divine beings, they close the heart down, thinking that they are protecting themselves. Isn't that interesting? What they are really doing is shutting themselves away from their support system, from all the Light, love and assistance that is available in the great network of consciousness that is the Divine Plan. As a defence mechanism, shutting down the heart doesn't work very well, does it?

Truly, opening the heart is the way to connect again. Through your heart you can reconnect into the great network that is there to support you and through it to the Source and to a recognition of your own Divinity. That is why it is important to work on opening the heart centre. That is also the reason that we begin all of our channelling exercises in the heart centre. What we are really saying is that we want to hear from all aspects of Self so that we can find the truth in its whole, complete form. You have all had experiences in which you decided to act from a rather narrow, singular focus and later found out that you had missed something, that there was another point of view that was at least as attractive or valid as the one that you were hanging on to so tightly. Perhaps it made you feel foolish because you did not act with the completeness that was possible for you. When you make your choices and act from the heart centre, this never happens.

When you have worked through the heart centre and you are able to blend all parts of yourself and all the knowledge that is there, you really step from knowledge into beingness. This truly is wisdom, isn't it? You know what the experience is all about because you are "being" in it.

Another important reason we want to keep working through the heart centre is to stretch it and open it so that you can receive and give all the wondrous qualities that the Source has made available to you. This includes, as I said earlier, unconditional love, acceptance, harmony, allowingness and other heart qualities that are a part of your support system. This support allows you to feel as though you can go forth and have adventures and really be bold and joyous. You will not be lost, separated or isolated. You will not fall out of things. You can grasp and leap as high as you desire. That is really important for evolution isn't it? If you are feeling so afraid and so isolated that you are unwilling to take the next step, you will probably find moving forward difficult and frightening. That is why it is so important to utilize the heart centre to draw in the support and to share it with others so that you all can feel the joy and courage of stepping forward in your evolution in love and Light.

Now of course, this is also very important for the Earth, isn't it? I think you realize that the Creator has a wondrous Plan for the Earth, a wonderful, wonderful opportunity for her to bring the qualities of the heart, the qualities of Divine love right into the physical world. That is an opportunity that is available to the Earth, an opportunity to bring forth into physicality beings of love and Light and to experience Divine creation from the heart focus, seeing it manifest in its beauty and balance. That is a wondrous service that is available to the Earth now. We are all working joyously in service to the Divine Plan in supporting the planet as she goes forth into her evolution, her wondrous opportunities.

This is one of the most important things that you are doing here. How do you actually do this? Well my friends, you begin by opening your own heart, by really allowing the Divine qualities of the heart to flow through you, giving and receiving them freely. You are part of the Earth right now and wherever you are, you are connected into her heart centre. Isn't that where we put the column of Light, right into the heart of the Earth? Accordingly, as you work with your own evolution, opening your heart so that you can bring through love and Light, you are sharing this energy with the Earth and participating in the grand design that is her present and future role within the cosmic Plan. In this way, service to Self and service to the Earth and the Divine Plan become one and the same process.

I think one of the best ways to open the heart is to focus on loving yourself. Now when I say that some people say to me, "Oh Vywamus, that sounds so difficult. How can I love myself? It is like hugging yourself. It really doesn't feel the same as hugging someone else." Truly, my friends, there is more to you than just the personality ego, isn't there? Why, you have a Soul and you have four bodies and you have other focuses that you can give and receive love to and from. I think that understanding the love that your Soul has for you and returning that love is a wonderful experience of self love. Truly it is. I would also like to tell you that self love is the most powerful protective force there is. Do you know that if you were completely at harmony within your heart and your energy were really deeply integrated through the heart centre and radiating very unconditionally the qualities of the heart, you wouldn't magnetize or draw to you any energy that is not as loving? I have told you many times that there really is a law of energy that says like attracts like. If you are radiating loving energy, if your aura is filled with love and the other qualities of the heart, what do you think you are going to draw to you? Certainly not attack, loneliness or pain. Becoming fully anchored and living moment to moment within the heart centre, giving and receiving all the wondrous qualities that are available through the heart centre from the Source, that is your greatest protection. Shutting down the heart centre to protect yourself doesn't really make much sense, does it?

CHANNELLING EXERCISE V
Opening the Heart Centre and Evolving
Self Through Communication

This exercise is intended to help you evolve yourself and to use the heart centre to find a blended truth for you on any given matter. What we are going to do is to find as many of the focuses or points of view that you are able to recognize within yourself and bring them all together to communicate, to share and to love each other. As these focuses learn to give and to receive together, the wonderful qualities of the heart will help you evolve into a beingness and knowingness that is complete. Again, I would like to remind you of what I have said several times earlier. These approaches that I am using in attempting to assist you in your growth are just that, approaches. They are not intended to describe what is real nor are they to be used as substitutes for reality. They are simply tools for understanding, no more, no less. When they no longer prove useful, they must be lovingly laid down. Then, the universe and your greater Self, seeing that you are complete with these aids, will send you new ones, better suited to the needs of your evolutionary progress. To view yourself as a collection of diverse and separate aspects, if taken as the truth about your inner reality, would distort and confuse your understanding of the wholeness and perfect integration of the beingness you truly are. At the same time, it can be very useful to imagine taking a wholeness apart, solely to examine and intimately get to know its notional parts. This can be quite helpful, particularly at the conceptual level, so long as you never loose sight of the truth that everything within you and without you is one great, seamless Whole. From this perspective, let us begin our meditative journey now.

Begin by relaxing and going within. See that you are in your golden column of Light and that you are deeply connected into the heart centre of the Earth. See also that your column goes upwards and is connected into the heart centre of the Source, heart to heart. You are a channel from the great heart of All That Is to the heart of the Earth. Feel now how this golden column of Light is strong, bright and clear and supports your connection into the Divine Plan, helping you to feel secure, supported, safe and wonderfully expansive.

Move into the heart centre, that wonderful place that we have been opening up and utilizing for all our channelling exercises. It is a lovely place, filled with beauty and the appreciation of all the wondrous experiences you have had in physicality. There is a lot of love here, my friends. Now we will repeat the exercise that we did previously with just the four bodies. You are seated at a wonderful long table and there are many chairs. They are all in the heart centre and you are sitting at one end of the table. You are the chairman of the board, and it is your responsibility to conduct the meeting, to make sure that all aspects of Self have a voice, are equal, loved and accepted here and that their truths are heard and respected. It is an important job for personality consciousness isn't it? At the other end of the table is the Soul. The Soul is there to help you to gather up all the truths and blend them into a whole. The Soul is very heart focused and it is part of the Soul's evolution to understand the importance of the heart centre and all the qualities of the heart. Indeed, my dear friends, your Souls have reached the stage in their evolution in which they understand this very well. They are now bringing this understanding through you to anchor it in the Earth and to help you to understand the wondrous opportunity that is available to you here upon this planet within the Divine Plan.

Just as you did in the four body exercise, use your imagination and bring into this room the four bodies, one at a time, first the physical body, then the emotional body, then the mental body and then the spiritual body. Remember that you are going to give them all wonderful colours and appearances and you are going to bring them in, welcome them and let them know how appreciated they are. When you have the four bodies nicely seated, I invite you to become aware that there is another knock at the door and that a new focus is seeking to come in. Some of you have already connected with this one. We are going to call it the heart focus. That's funny isn't it, because you are already in the heart centre. There really is also a point of view that is a heart focused point of view. It is the point of view that comes from all those wonderful heart qualities like unconditional love, harmony, gratitude, allowingness and the others that we have talked about. You will soon see that each one of your focuses, the four bodies and all others that are going to come, all have heart centres of their own. They are what we call holographic. That means that they are replicas of the whole of you just as you are holographic, containing all the aspects of the Wholeness within you. As you evolve, more and more of your Divinity comes forth. Each one of these bodies and focuses have aspects just like you, and they all have heart centres. So this consciousness, this focus that we call the heart focus is really a kind of composite that has blended the qualities of the heart from the physical body, the emotional body, the mental body, the spiritual body and the other focus that you are utilizing now and are going to consciously get to know. Welcome this new focus in the same way you have done the others, giving it wondrous colours and a beautiful appearance to reflect its supportive function in your own evolution within the Divine Plan.

After you have the heart focus seated in a comfortable chair and have made it feel welcome, become aware that there is another knock at the door. I think that this time we will bring in your will or intention centre. You know that this is a very important part of Self, because if you can't get the will or intention to agree to something it is very much like fighting uphill. Perhaps you have sometimes wondered why, although you had mentally decided to do something, you just couldn't seem to get committed to it. You tried and tried and tried but somehow you couldn't seem to bring all of your energies to bear. Often, this was because the will or intention focus had really not agreed, had not accepted what you had decided to do.

You can see how important it is to bring this focus into connection with all the others so that when you decide to do something important in your life, the will/intention focus will commit its strong and powerful energies in support of what you have decided. Now bring this one in and give it colours and an appearance that reflect its importance, its strength, its decisiveness. It is very decisive and can be a very clear energy when it is powerfully committed to something. It is through this focus that you can hold powerfully present in your life your connection to the Source and, more importantly, to your own Divinity.

Now we have six focuses around the table, four bodies, the heart focus and will focus. There is another focus that is very important to you right now. We will call it the Earth focus, or the planetary connection focus. Become aware that this focus is knocking at the door, seeking to come in. It is by means of this focus that you are able to integrate into the energetic field of the planet, so that you can sustain yourself in physicality through an understanding of the principles and opportunities and the way in which life is expressed herein. This focus can tell you a great deal about your relationship with the Earth and you know already that this is a very important thing, particularly for physical health. As well, it can aid your understanding of your purposeful service to the Earth. Please give your Earth connection some colours and a wondrous appearance that reflects its service to Self in physicality, to the Earth and to the Creator's Plan as it is reflected in physicality. Show it to a seat at your table and make it very welcomed, accepted and loved. This is good practice in expressing love for Self, don't you think?

I think you are going to find that there is another focus knocking at the door in your heart. This one I like to call your cosmic connection, although sometimes it has other names. It is the focus of you that is very much a partner to your Earth focus. It helps you to stay connected to All That Is, all the other aspects of Sourceness, all the other focuses and realms of consciousness. This focus helps you to stay connected into the Galactic Core so that you can experience your physicality deeply but without feeling disconnected or cut off from the rest of Creation or from the Source. It helps you to connect with the Space Brothers, for example. I think this one really has a very expansive energy as it helps you to feel connected into that wonderful support system and to all the joyous adventures that are happening around you in Creation. Bring this focus in and give it colours and

*an appearance that reflect its expansiveness, its connected-
ness and all the wondrous adventures and excitement that
are available through this particular focus. Please give it a
seat around the table and make it feel loved, accepted and
very welcome. You might thank it for coming and thank all
the others too. Remember, you, as the personality ego, are
the chairman of the board. It is through you that all these
focuses come to understand that they are all unique and
special, equally valuable in their contribution to the evolution of Self, the planet and the Divine Plan, and, at the same
time, united together as a fully integrated wholeness.*

*I would like you to bring in the next two focuses together.
As I view it, they represent the creative flow as it expresses
itself in dynamic and receptive energies or what you like to
call masculine and feminine qualities. The creative flow is
just a wonderful kind of flow that moves from the Source for
the purposes of creation. It is part of the Divine Plan. It
seems to me that this Source has arranged things so that
creating will be done through two streams or lines of force,
masculine and feminine or dynamic and receptive. I like to
see them as coming in together because they really are
branches of the same energy. See that they are standing at
the door to your heart and are seeking entry. Please give
them appearances and colours that really reflect their
creativity, the excitement and power for thrusting of the
masculine and the receptive wisdom, connectedness and
strength of the feminine. Also take into account the
equalities that really suggest themselves. Bring them in and
find them a place at the table. Make them feel loved,
accepted and welcomed.*

*There is another focus knocking at the door to your heart. I
think you will find that this is number eleven. This one can
have several different names. This channel has chosen to
see that she has a focus for the subconscious/unconscious*

mind and that is quite alright, but a different one will perhaps present itself to many of you. You have had lots of practice in imagining the appearances of your focuses. What colours come to mind for this next one? Give it an appearance that seems to be appropriate but first I think you may wish to ask it, "What focus of me are you? What talents and abilities do you have? What part of me are you?" If you have some difficulty getting this information, ask the Soul to help. Remember, this is a channelling exercise and you are giving the words and voice to each one. When you have understood who this focus is, and you have stabilized its colours and appearance, give it a seat around the table. Make it feel welcomed, accepted and loved.

We have eleven focuses gathered in your heart centre now. If any other aspect seems to present itself and asks to be a part of this, consult the Soul and, if it seems appropriate, welcome and seat them as well. Let us proceed at this time with our eleven focuses and the Soul. Perhaps we should say that we have twelve, including the conscious self. This is the ego personality level and I think it would be very useful if you gave yourself as this aspect an appearance and a lovely cloak of your favourite colours. It is important to realize that the personality, that you sometimes call the ego, is an extremely important part of Self too. So often people think that as they become more spiritual they are supposed to destroy or let go of the ego. I really don't think this is quite accurate, at least in so far as physicality is concerned. I think you have spent a lot of time evolving a strong, efficient personality Self so that it can be of service to the Soul and to the larger Self as a whole. In this exercise it is the chairman of the board whose task it is to ensure that all the focuses of Self understand their uniqueness and their equality. As conscious Self, you have invited them all here with the Soul and it is you who will often be the one to suggest the problems and concerns which they will all be considering *and discussing.*

At this point, I think that you may wish to invite one or more of the Spiritual Teachers to join you and to assist with the process. Ask your Soul to help invoke their presence and then put forth your invitation. I think that you quickly will notice that there is a knocking in your heart centre at the door to the Spiritual Plane. When you open the door you will see that standing there is the Teacher you have invoked. Show them to a seat at the table and welcome them. When this is done, I think it is very important to introduce all the focuses to the Soul and to the Spiritual Teacher.

Now, what happens next? That is up to you. I like to call this exercise "the round table." You can bring any problem or question to this table and ask each focus of Self to speak about their perspective or point of view on the matter you have raised. You can go around the table encouraging each one to speak freely. As well, I think it is important to emphasize that each one's truth is equally important and equally part of the whole. You really will want to put personality's perspective in there too. When you are finished, the Soul will then stand up and summarize and blend together lovingly and allowingly what every one has said. I am sure that you will see that a wondrous truth, a whole truth, a truth that you can experience as a part of your beingness will come forth. The Soul will assist you to blend the energies and the points of view expressed so that everyone will be right and no one will be wrong or left out.

I believe that you can process almost any question or concern in this way. There is so much wisdom within your beingness. What we are doing in this exercise is learning to use the communicative patterning of relating from consciousness to consciousness that is at the core of the Divine Plan. This really does support and assist your evolution. If you do this often, you will find that you can move forward in all aspects of your life with a far more balanced and whole perspective. From my point of view, I really don't think that there is anything too trivial or too traumatic to ask for a solution that is whole, a solution that really embodies the totality of who and what you are as a Divine Being. Allow this exercise to evolve in any way that seems appropriate. If you are confused at any time or have some difficulty with the exercise, ask your Soul and the Spiritual Teachers that you work with to help you. You know that you can always call on me, Vywamus, at any time and I will be there for you immediately. It would be a great joy and privilege for me if you were to do so.

When you are completely finished with the exercise, return fully into your physical body. Occupy it completely and then begin to release any extra channelled energy through your feet down into your column of Light, into the heart of the Earth. Let the energy flow from the top of your head all the way down through your body and out your feet. As this energy flows from you down into the Earth see how the heart of the Earth responds to you, sending back a beautiful, nurturing, emerald green/gold Light that is clear, warm and sweet. It flows through your body, nurturing you and filling you with warmth, love and support from the Earth. See how this Earth energy flows up through the top of your head out into the column of Light and upwards, connecting into the heart of the Source. Feel the loving connection that you are facilitating. Now, allow yourself to rest in this column of Light, supported by the Source Light and the Earth's nurturing energy. Rest there until you feel strong, complete and peaceful.

I would like to end this chapter by reminding you that it is very important that you make these exercises your own. If, in the course of them you are presented in your inner vision with a different visualization than the one I have suggested in this writing, always, always go with that which your inner wisdom is providing to you. That is a key part of self love, to prefer and to adopt your own truth over the truth of another, even when that other appears to have some special position of knowledge, as you sometimes think we Spiritual Teachers do. If, in this last exercise, you are introduced to ten aspects of Self or Thirteen or they describe themselves as being different from the aspect I have included in the writing, it is absolutely necessary to go with your own inner wisdom and to allow it to evolve the meditation that I have given into something that is uniquely your own. To prefer my vision of reality over your own would be deeply disempowering to you and that certainly is the opposite of my intent in writing this book. This choosing to follow your own wisdom over that of others is a key truth for all of life as well.

CHAPTER 5

Healing Through Communication

In this chapter, I would like to help you to support your physical structure. I call this lesson "Healing Through Communication". I have talked a lot about communication and you will remember that one of the things I have said is that this Source's Plan is really based on a communicative pattern. It involves different divine focuses communicating with each other, sharing energy and experience and, through that communicative process, evolving each other and thereby the Source. I think that communication is something that works for almost any difficulty you may encounter. The exercise I will give you is very good for helping to heal health problems that have arisen but that is not the only thing that you can do with it. It is also a fine way to give your body consciousness support and nurturing which is an ongoing part of loving yourself.

I think that you will find that you are really forging ahead in your evolution and growing spiritually. Did you know that this means that you are going to grow physically as well? Stop and think about it for a moment. As you expand spiritually, your structure is going to get bigger (I don't mean fatter, so don't worry), that is to say, larger in terms of energetic capability, stronger and brighter. As well, your body consciousness is going to start operating on some new principles. At times this may be a little hard for some of you to accept, but you will notice over the next several years that what I say is true.

One of the first things that you have told us that you would like to do with your physical body is to stop the aging process. You really don't have to get old you know. It is another one of those beliefs that is part of the way your body consciousness is programmed at the D.N.A. level. It is entirely possible to change that. Perhaps you have thought that it would be much better if you could use a physical structure for as long as you wanted and then, when you didn't need it any more, you could just release it lovingly and consciously. Wouldn't it be nice if it was in good working condition the whole time you wanted to dwell within it? I think that is a very worthwhile goal. In fact, that is what is happening within humanity at this time. As you change your perspective, as you become more aware of yourself as Divine beings that really are unlimited, you begin to anchor that understanding deeply at all levels of yourself. Your structure is going to be the body of an unlimited being of Light instead of that of a small, lonely, separated creature. That has been the structure that humanity has been using for quite some time now.

As you step into your mastery of the physical world, for that is what it is all about - becoming a master of your own life and your own process, probably you would like to have things a little different-ly arranged in your physical structure. This is something that you can work on very consciously. However, I do want to let you know that it is going to happen anyway, because, as you expand, as you bring in more Light, as your vibrational level goes up, of course it is going to affect your physical structure. You all have been moving quite rapidly in your evolution lately. This is partly because of the way the Earth is accelerating her own movement into the next planetary evolutionary cycle. This creates a flowing of energy that moves anybody that wants to move forward much faster than they used to be able to do. It is not a "one foot in front of the other" kind of proposition any more. As you move in this way, many of you are pressing yourselves rather extensively. You are pushing your physical body to change quite rapidly and comprehensively as well.

The physical body changes start at the cellular level. They are now being activated within the glandular network, as parts of your structure that you haven't yet used fully awaken. I think you know that the scientists of your planet have discovered, for example, that you are really not using all of your brain. I think everybody knows that. Did you ever wonder what you are supposed to be doing with the rest of the brain? Well I am happy to tell you that you are going to find out. You are already finding out. There are capabilities within the mind/brain structure that are for channelling and for directing the creation of your structure in a more purposeful way. There are circuits in the brain/mind complex which direct that capability which you have called the third eye and all those other capabilities that you have labelled "psychic".

I think that most of you have accepted that these abilities are latent in all of humanity. What does latent mean? I think it means "sleeping". What do you do with something that is sleeping that you really would like to be able to use? You activate it. How is that done? Well, you bring in a lot of energy and you wake it up. That gets us back to channelling doesn't it? You are waking up the sleeping capabilities that are a part of your structure, part of the way the Creator envisions the human structure to be. Some of them have been sleeping for quite awhile, and you are not aware that they are part of who you are.

This awakening begins to happen as you start to anchor in your dense physical structure the energetic power of the whole Self. Many people still believe within their core realities that "spiritual" energy is too refined, too perfect, to be effectively integrated into the Earth plane. They continually focus on extending themselves into the "higher dimensions" rather than directing their efforts towards expressing their divinity through their physical world and conscious-ness. You can hold your "spirituality" out of the physical body if you wish but, in doing so, you cheat yourself of the fullness of living that is the Earth's gift to you. What we are talking about is bringing your divine Self deeply into the body and, through it, into the Earth. As this begins to happen, it activates your structure and the latent capabilities and ideal patterns that are hidden there, hidden in your DNA.

One of the things that happens as you activate new programming is that you have to deal with the old programming. Some of it you will want to keep, for example, information as to how to utilize the nutrients that are on the Earth for your physical health. However, some of the physical programming isn't very useful and I think ageing is one of those arrangements that you will be willing to let go. In order to bring in a new program, you are going to want to make room by letting go some of the old.

Between the time when you are letting go of the old programs that have supported your structure for thousands and thousands of years and many, many lifetimes, and before the new programming is truly working and visible for you to see and to become comfortable with, there is a kind of in between phase that sometimes feels strange. At times, your body starts to feel that things are changing so fast that it cannot be comfortable any more. Much of this changing is chemical because that's the way that your physical structure works. Much of your chemistry is controlled by your glandular structure. One of the areas that we activate through the channelling process is the pineal/pituitary complex within your brain/mind structure. You could say that it is the captain of the ship. The increase in your vibrational rate within the pineal/pituitary complex activates those higher glandular functions and they in turn send out new commands to the rest of the glandular network and, through it, to the other body systems. New chemical reactions are stimulated. Old chemical reactions begin to be phased out.

This means your body chemistry is going to go through some changes, and some of your organs are going to feel insecure. Did you know that organs can feel insecure? I think you know what it feels like to have an insecure heart, for example, or a liver that feels a little shaky about its function and everyone knows what it feels like to have fearful intestines or a digestive system that lacks confidence and strength. During these changes your structure needs help, needs strengthening, comfort and support. How are we going to arrange that? I know you are all thinking, "Good grief! He wants me to start talking to my feet, or my ears or my liver". That's just what I want you to do, although I don't think we will start with your ears, but if you like, we can.

What I am really saying is that we need to address the issue of separation. Pain comes from separation. Whenever you are having pain or disfunction you are experiencing a manifestation of separation. That part of you that is in pain is feeling separated from the rest of you. The energy does not flow freely to and from that part. That part is not feeling balanced and connected. Its functioning is not aligned with the rest of you. Some persons who practice healing talk about bringing your body back into alignment. To me, alignment is a lot like agreement. Everyone lines up together and agrees on the same points of view and functions according to the same harmonious principles. So when part of you is in pain, feeling out of alignment and a little separated, you can do something about it yourself. Let's look at an example. When you have someone in your group that is feeling unhappy, separated, isolated and locked out, what do you do about that? I think communicating with them, giving them love, acceptance and support to help them in whatever it is that they are going through works quite well. What you are doing is giving them energy, the energy of love and support. This heart centered energy brings about some wonderful things here on the physical plane.

This is what I think you can do to help your physical structure. It really isn't hard at all. I want you to use your imagination because I know that you never expected to channel your own liver or your heart. Think about it for a minute. What did I say channelling is? I said that it is just receiving pulses of energy and translating them into words and concepts that you can understand. I don't see why you can't channel the vibrational frequency of one of your organs. I am sure that you all realize that your heart puts out pulses of energy and that sometimes the pulses could be interpreted to say, "Everything is working very well. I am feeling extremely harmonious and comfortable and I really enjoy supporting the physical structure in this way." I think you could imagine your heart putting out those kind of energy pulses, and I think that you could also imagine energy pulses coming from your heart that say, "Help! I need support. I feel weak and unnurtured. I don't think I can bear this burden. I don't think I can do my job if I cannot get more support." I think that you can imagine your heart putting out energy pulses that could be interpreted in that way.

I know also that you all realize that each and every cell, every organ and every tissue in your body is intelligent and conscious and vibrates with its own unique frequency as a part of the divine Whole. Everything within you and without you is expressing its own vision of this wholeness and is communicating ceaselessly   Understanding this communication and responding to it is simply a matter of tuning in with your own divine awareness. I have always said that the imagination is the pathway to higher knowingness and I have encouraged everyone to use their imagination in the search for truth. This exercise that I am now giving to you is going to be imaginative, because you will personify a particular part of your body consciousness and tune into its vibration to find out what it has been trying to say to you.

What do you do if you find out that, for example, your heart is saying, "I need support"? I think it would be appropriate to ask your Soul. I think you are all getting used to the idea that the Soul really does have answers. It sends out energy pulses that communicate with you and that you can interpret very well into words. Also, of course, there are the Spiritual Teachers. Some of them are very helpful and extremely good at working with physical structures. I, Vywamus, have made quite a study of the human physical consciousness and am learning more about it as I work with those of you who dwell in one. That is why I feel that I have some expertise in the area of channelling, because I know how to help your structure to accept energy that comes from a different vibrational level without discomfort or fear.

CHANNELLING EXERCISE VI
Healing Through Communication

We will begin in the same way we always begin. We are going to reference your column of Light. Go within and see that you are surrounded by a golden column of Light. You are completely in that golden Light. Focus your attention below your feet and see that this beautiful column of Light goes straight down, unbroken and smooth to connect with the heart of the Earth. Shift your focus of attention and see that this column of Light reaches up above your head, right up to the Source of all things, so high that you cannot imagine anything higher. It goes right into a great white Light that truly symbolizes your Source connection. See how this column of beautiful golden Light is unbroken, connecting from the heart of the Source down around and through your structure and deep down into the heart of the Earth. Feel that you are in the Light and supported by the Light as you now work in your channel. This is a representation of the energy that your channel truly is, and it is also a visualization of your connection and commitment to the Source and to the Earth.

See that your conscious mind is like a little figure of Light centred in your head and see that descending before you is a beautiful set of stairs. Descend these stairs. They are bright and beautiful and full of Light and you move down them joyously. When you come to the bottom of the stairs, you enter into a glorious room, right at the heart centre. This is a wonderful multi-dimensional place that connects you to All That Is.

As we have done in earlier exercises, see that all the focuses of Self are seated around a great table. Your four bodies are there and the other focuses that you have come to recognize as being a part of you. The Soul is there, shining in its Light, beautiful, glorious, loving and completely committed to your highest and best good. You, as conscious personality Self, are the chairman of the board. You are the one who must organize things. If you would like to have a Spiritual Teacher join you in this communicative exercise, invoke that your Teacher come forth from the Spiritual Plane. Notice once more with your imagination the door you have within this beautiful room that has the sign on it saying, "This is the Door to the Spiritual Plane." See now that someone is knocking at your door. Move to the door and open it. Standing on the threshold is the Teacher that you have called. Invite your Teacher in and give them a seat at your table.

You will remember that we always begin these channelling exercises with a very clear statement of intention. For as clear as your statement is, that is the power of the commitment and the energy that you put forth into actualizing the goal you are seeking. The purpose of this particular exercise is to communicate with a part of your physical structure. Think for a moment. What part of the physical structure would you like to get to know better? What part would you like to understand and give support to? Think about it now. When you have decided, please stand up and make a very clear statement of your intention to everyone that is seated at the table so that all can hear what it is that you are going to do now. I think that if there is some concern or problem that you want to focus upon, it is wise to state that too. Fully energize your invocation and include in your statement as many details as you feel are appropriate. At this point, see with your imagination that all of the focuses of Self that are sitting at the table are in agreement that this is a very worthwhile quest. If any part does not seem to be in agreement, pause, and with the help of the Soul, respond to the concerns raised. Then see that all your focuses signal their agreement by gathering their energy and blending their vibrations and colours right into the Soul energy. Allow yourself as personality focus also to blend into the Soul energy and now you become one great glowing body of Light, whole, complete and strong in your intention. You are focused, balanced and aligned into this purpose that you have set forth.

Feel yourself in the energy of your Soul with your Spiritual Teacher moving to another door that you begin to see forming in one of the walls. The door has Light of whatever colour that seems appropriate to you flowing around its edges. As you come closer to the door, see that it has a little sign on it that reads, "This is the Way to the Physical Structure."

Reach out with your energy hands and open the door. Use your imagination and see yourself stepping over the threshold. See that the Spiritual Teacher that you have called upon is coming with you. See that before you is a corridor. It is bright and filled with Light and has many flowing colours. Light sparkles off the walls, the floor and ceiling and it flows all around you. If you find this corridor perhaps a little dim when you first move along it, see that the Light of your Soul consciousness brightens it up gloriously and you can truly see the beauty that surrounds you. Continue down the corridor. You notice that your journey seems to be taking you in the direction of the physical location that you have desired to connect with.

Now you can see that the corridor comes to an end and there is an opening. The ceiling is higher and the walls open up so that you see that there is a door. For some of you, the door will look quite ancient, as though it has been locked or unopened for a long time. For others, the door will look as though it has been used many times. Use your imagination. Does this door look like it has been used? Is the path well travelled, or does it look like it has been a long, long time since you have consciously passed through this door? Let us open the door, but before you do, remember that you are cradled within the energy of your Soul. You are whole, supported, loved and complete. You are really very strong and joyous and you know that the Light of the Soul will energize the whole process. In your Soul energy you can deal with anything that needs your attention and your love. See that your Spiritual Teacher also is there with you, guiding, assisting and supporting you with love and Light. Reach out with your energy hands and open the door. Perhaps it is difficult. Maybe the hinges creak. Notice if it was easy to open or difficult.

Perhaps at first it will seem a little dark inside the door. Step inside now and see immediately that the Light of the Soul brightens up this place. It is no longer dark. Look around. Use your imagination to see what this place is like, for it truly is the place within your structure with which you are seeking to connect. It has certain qualities, colours and textures. It has a specific kind of energy and perhaps a little gloom as well. What do you see? Does it look like everything is working very well? Does it look as if there is enough energy or a lot of energy flowing? Does it look a little dark? Do not worry. The Soul will support you in all the work that you need to do here. It is going to be quite easy. So allow yourself to truly see what is here to be seen and support this with your imagination. Perhaps you might even have an image that will come forth from another time or another life. Just accept whatever comes forth, for there is knowledge and wisdom here for you if you will open to receive it.

See that there is a figure in a corner off to one side. It is a human figure. Use you imagination. How is it dressed? Is it brightly coloured? Is its garment rich, bright and full of colours or dark and tattered? Look now. Use your imagination. Is the figure tall or short? Is it thin or very plump? Is the face hidden? See that it begins to notice that you are here. Maybe you will have to go over to it and speak to it. Of course, the first thing it is going to say is, "Who are you? What are you doing here?" That's what you would say, if this was your place and a being of Light came along.

I think that it is an appropriate time to introduce yourself. I think it is quite alright to say your present Earth name and you might say that you are coming to see it and that you believe it is really a part of the consciousness of your physical body. I think it would also be very appropriate to explain that the Light which surrounds you is the Light of the Soul and of the whole Self and that you are here to give love and support. You might want to introduce your Spiritual Teacher if you have brought one. Then ask this consciousness, this figure, "How are you?" Ask it to explain what is going on in this part of your body consciousness. How is it functioning? Is there a problem or any need or request it has? You will really want to stress that you and the Soul have wonderful resources to assist and aid this part of you in its functioning.

Discuss this now. Give words to the energy that this one is emitting to you. See it as a person speaking to you. Use your imagination. There is a lot of wisdom here if you are willing to receive it. In the course of this conversation you are having, I think it is very important to ask this part of you what it really would like to have and what it needs. It is also very important for you to attempt to understand as completely as you can what is being communicated. If you are having difficulty, ask your Soul for some input. Please give all the participants in this exercise words to communi-

cate with each other.

At this point I think the Soul has a wonderful gift for this part of the body consciousness, and perhaps so does the Spiritual Teacher that is with you. Use your imagination and see what is being given. It may be that what is needed is a releasing. It may be that this part of you is holding old ideas, fears, pains or memories of these things or a sense of unworthiness and limitedness. I think you will find that there is some old programming to release here so that the gift of the new that the Soul brings can truly be anchored. So if you can see that something needs releasing attempt to understand and express what it is.

When you have true understanding of this, begin the releasing process. See that there is a violet flame that your Soul is holding, a beautiful violet flame with the power of transmutation. Using your imagination, see that this old energy that needs releasing is present and has an appearance and colour. Repressed fear, pain, separation and unworthiness have dark colours that you can imagine quite easily. See that you can pull them right out of this part of you. Perhaps you can reach in to this physical consciousness and gently relieve it of this heavy energy. Before doing so, ask for its help, consent and understanding of what is going on and then release this dark and dense energy into the violet flame. See it transmuting and burning gloriously until it is completely burned away and turned into sparks of brilliant white Light that surround you and this part of your physical consciousness. Perhaps there will be a cloak of new energy or a crown of Light or a rod of power that is to be given to this part of your body. Whatever it is symbolizes the new energy, the new program for this part of you.

See with your inner seeing that, as this aspect of your physical consciousness receives all this wonderful energy, it begins to transform into beauty and Light with flowing joyous colours. Its appearance is changing and its energy is harmonizing. See how the environment in which you found this consciousness is changing too. It is becoming lighter and brighter and perhaps you will allow the violet flame to move around the whole area, lighting up and consuming anything that is dark or dull and transmuting it into bright, sparkling Light.

I think it would be very appropriate if we brought down a vortex of beautiful rainbow colours, bright, electrical and sparkling. See your Soul as bringing it in now. Allow this vortex of rainbow colours to sweep all around the whole of this place and to sweep you and the physical consciousness. Feel this area expanding with the Light and joy of transformation. See that this vortex of rainbow Light goes out through the floor and imagine that it moves right down through your column of Light into the heart of the Earth where it is anchored. All that was dark or dense is transformed into beautiful Light that serves the Earth very well.

At this time, I have a suggestion. I think that this part of you would enjoy it if you were to hook up a line of communication into your heart centre. You can use your imagination. I suppose it would be very easy to imagine that you were putting in a new telephone or, if you like to communicate through crystals, you could set them up as well. In whatever way seems appropriate to you, set up this two way line of communication between the heart centre and this place in your physical structure. Explain to this part of you that this truly is a communication device and that it can use the device to communicate with you and with the Soul whenever it wishes to be heard, to ask for love and support or just to experience the connection more fully.

We are going to go back up the corridor through which we

came but I think that it would be very nice if you brought this part of you along. It will be alright. Certainly enough energy will remain to perform the functions that it has been performing. I would like you to show it your beautiful heart centre so that it feels a little more a part of everything. Go back through the door now. Remember that you are travelling within your Soul energy and with your Spiritual Teacher. See yourself moving up the corridor, gliding along, seeing the Light, colour and beauty of this corridor as it is lit up by the Light of your Soul and your conscious presence. Bringing this physical consciousness focus with you, come back through the door into the heart centre. Show this part of your physical consciousness around the heart centre and explain what the heart centre really is and what you do here. Show it the other end of its communication line, perhaps another telephone or crystal, whatever you have set up. Help this part of you to feel truly connected and part of the whole beingness that guides your life.

If you are using your imagination well, you will see quite clearly how delighted this part of you is to be connected in this way, to be part of who you really are. When this is complete, allow this focus to return through the corridor back to its place in the consciousness of your physical structure. Give it love. Let it know that you will be there for it with support, love and Light. Rest now within the heart centre, still supported by the energy of the Soul. Perhaps you and your Soul and your Spiritual Teacher would like to discuss what you have discovered. If it is not entirely clear to you what has happened, if you have not fully realized what you have discovered, ask them to explain it a little more fully and to aid in a full understanding and integration of this process.

I think you will find that quite often you will want to repeat this exercise and to take as much time as you need. The *goal is to reach as full an understanding of the nature and function of the physical structure and as complete an alignment with your ideal energetic patterning as is available to you at this time. You can use this exercise for any part of you and I recommend that you do it often to support your physical consciousness while it is going through these wonderful changes. You will find that you have much less difficulty physically if you do. You will truly become aware that you are a whole being that is completely conscious in its beingness and its growth.*

When you are complete with the exercise, release the channelled energy within your body. Feel it flowing down from the top of your head, moving down through your feet and into the Earth. Feel the Earth's loving response to you as a beautiful, nurturing, emerald green/gold energy flows softly up the column of Light into your body. This soft, vibrant Earth energy flows upward through your structure and moves up in the column of Light to merge into the heart of the Source. Allow yourself to feel the joyous connection that you are facilitating. Feel yourself fully present in your physical body and when you are ready, open your eyes.

EVOLUTIONARY EXERCISES for CHANNELS

CHAPTER 6
Past Life Regression

We are going to have a wonderful adventure in this chapter. We are going to give you an exercise whereby you can, well, the term that you sometimes like to use is, "regress yourself" into a past life. I know that many of you have thought, "Well, why should I bother? What good are my past lives to me? They are gone. What truly concerns me is this life I am living now." I would like to say to you that many of your past experiences are not as truly gone as you might think because they have come forward in terms of energy to act out again the same story but this time in your present life. These are often causal in actions that you take that you had not consciously intended or chosen. Sometimes you notice that you seem to make decisions that come out the same way over and over again, yet you really could not see when you were initiating them how they were part of a repeating pattern and you do not understand how you could have chosen to act it out again.

Some of you may even have noticed that there are quite a number of such patterns in your life, very unsatisfying ones, that keep repeating but you can't seem to remember where you first picked them up. Frequently, you have acquired them in another life. Consequently, letting them go in this life is somewhat more difficult unless you are able to go back and understand some of the decisions and judgements you made at the time that brought this habit into existence or this pattern into your life. Sometimes you are really stuck in the past and it is like a broken record. It keeps going over and over the same track, but the track is larger than one life. It is a track that comes forward from several lives in the past and is stored in the D.N.A. until it is activated in the present and begins to play out all over again. Sometimes, because of the emotional intensity that surrounds some of these types of experiences in the present, it is easier to look for their roots in your past lives and to view them somewhat more objectively from the perspective of the greater evolutionary wisdom and maturity that you have acquired since that time.

I also have observed that, if you are dealing with a particularly comprehensive pattern of beliefs and accompanying emotions, the distortions that it has created in your life and in your self identity release and integrate quite easily, once the original root cause and misunderstanding is identified and resolved in the past life context in which it first took hold in your energetic structure. As well, I have found that your Soul, if asked, will unerringly guide you back along your life paths just as far as is appropriate, taking into account the issue you are focusing on and the degree of intensity that you are able to deal with comfortably at the time.

This is a channelling exercise so we ask you to channel. You will see the persons involved within your inner vision and you will have the full support of your Soul and Spiritual Teacher in the process. You are the one who must give them their words because they will certainly communicate, but their communication will be in the form of energy pulses. It will be your words and concepts that must be fitted to those pulses and you will be very much like an actor that goes first to one part and speaks one character's lines and then to the next part and speaks that character's lines. You will be a very talented actor. You will be a "one man show", you might say. Make no mistake, the energies are very real. You are merely the one that gives them a voice. Consequently, you are practising your channelling while you are doing this.

CHANNELLING EXERCISE VII
Past Life Regression

Begin this exercise by referencing your golden channel of Light that you see is all around you, beautiful and bright. See that it penetrates below your feet, deep into the heart of the Earth, strong, solid and very connected. Allow yourself to feel very comfortable and solid, and then focus on how your column of Light extends right up into the heart of the Source level itself. When you look up with your inner seeing, you can see far, far up this golden column that at the very top is a bright, white Light, so bright that it is beyond imagining. You know it is your connection to the Source. You see that your column of Light is completely unbroken. There are no breaks or gaps and you are fully protected, supported and in peaceful solitude within the wholeness of the Self. Everything you see and experience will be in the Light and you will be comfortable throughout the whole exercise.

Now, see with your imagination that your conscious self is like a little human figure of bright Light that is sitting in the middle of your head. Draw your conscious focus into that point inside of your head until your whole conscious awareness is fully centered in that place. See that there is a beautiful staircase in front of you, golden and crystalline, that gently winds downward. You walk down this staircase, enjoying the Light and beauty all around you. You come out at the bottom into your heart centre.

The heart centre is that marvellous place where you have stored all the beauty and excitement that you have experienced in your journey in physicality. Using your imagination, give it some detail and solidness. Give it beautiful furniture and a lovely, high bright ceiling and many lights and colours. See once again the large table around which all your focuses, your four bodies and the other aspects of which you have become aware, are sitting. They are excited because they have heard that you are going on a wonderful, magical adventure into history, your history, the history of your evolution. See how delighted they are. They are all ready to go. This is just going to be fun!

See now that your Soul is present. It very beautiful, filled with Light and joy. Your Soul is promising you that it will be with you throughout the whole adventure, supporting you and helping you to understand what it is that you are seeing and learning in this exercise. Remember, you are going to be channelling the wisdom of the Soul, and bringing the Light of the whole Self into these experiences and these lives that have gone before. Some of them do need a little more Light in order to be understood and integrated into your understanding of who you truly are as a divine being.

Perhaps, there is a Spiritual Teacher that you would like to bring with you. Use your imagination now and see the door that has the writing on it that says, "This Way to the Spiritual Plane". You know, I think you will hear a knocking at the door. It is your Spiritual Teacher coming to help you with your exciting adventure. Go to the door and open it. See with your inner vision that your friend and Spiritual Teacher is standing there, smiling at you, and saying, "I heard that you are going to take a wonderful adventure into a past life so that you can have knowledge and learning from this experience. I want to come with you and support and help you, if you will allow me". Are you going to invite this dear friend to come with you? Yes, I think so. Welcome this Teacher into the heart centre.

Gather up all the focuses of the Self who are so anxious to be a part of this journey and see them now merging into the energy of the Soul. You feel your whole Self merging now into this greater, more comprehensive level of being. You can feel that your Soul is holding you there like a very precious gem within a beautiful flower of Light. You are safe, secure, supported and loved in the Soul energy. Remember, everything you do and see now will come through the Light and love of this expansive perspective.

You are now ready to set of on your quest. See that another door is forming in a different wall in your heart centre room. Come closer and look at the door. There is writing on it as well, a sign, and it says, "This Way to the Lives That I Have Lived". Well, that's pretty clear, isn't it. I, Vywamus, would like to come. I would like to come because I think that I am a helpful communicator. If you would like to have my assistance throughout the journey, just say, "Vywamus, I want you to come and help me find appropriate words. Help me with my channelling so that I can understand everyone that wants to speak to me and give them all the words and concepts that they need to communicate with me". This is all that you have to do and I will come and help you. You don't have to see me or even know me very well, but you will feel that someone is there helping you to be clear, to hear what is being said, to understand it and to find the right words to give each one a voice. I would also like to offer you the support of my energy and my love.

If you are willing to proceed now, stand before the door and state very clearly your intention. You may wish to specify a particular life you are aware of or merely to ask to see the lifetime that will best assist you to understand and clear in a particular area. Are you asking to see a life in which you think that a problem might have occurred that you could release there and help with your present life? Is it a life which might assist you to answer the question, "Did I know this person in my present life before?" Perhaps you will just say, "I would like to know if I lived in Atlantis or some other wonderful civilization like Egypt." Maybe you will say, "I *want to know if I have ever been a channel before. Please show me a life in which I was and everything went well." If you are feeling stuck with your channelling, perhaps you will say, "I would like to see a life in which I was a channel before but where I collected the problem that is affecting my channelling today. I want to go back and have a look."*

In the exercise that I am now going to lead you through, I will be focusing on assisting you in resolving a problem or difficulty in your present life which has its roots in an experience in the past that was difficult or painful and was not able to be fully integrated or completed in that previous life. I am focusing on this objective because it is the one that people most often ask me to assist them with. This does not mean that this is the only use for the exercise. Indeed, this is not the case at all. The process can be used to journey to what I have sometimes called "lives of power". These are past lives in which you have been able to form a very strong and creative persona who has had great success in meeting the goals or purposes you set for yourself before entering into the life. Perhaps you were a great artist or musician or a successful and respected leader. You may have been a very clear and joyous channel or have lived and loved very greatly. Lives like that hold immense power and wisdom which you can get more consciously in touch with by remembering who you have been and seeing the greatness and creativity that you have already been able to manifest in the past.

So you see that you have many choices. Let us now continue with your journey. Stand before the door for a few moments and clarify what it is you are seeking. Be sure you are very, very clear about what you want, because your clarity is what is going to take you to the right place. What you are doing is telling your Soul which life to show you. Your Soul knows all of the lives you have already experienced.

When this is complete, open the door and step through with your Soul and Spiritual Teacher. See that you are standing in a long, long corridor. Go down the corridor. See that it is a beautiful corridor, very ornate. There is gold and crystal on the walls and floor. There are many beautiful colours, but the doors are not activated. It is as though they are sleeping. You glide down the corridor for a period of time until you suddenly see that one of the doors is beginning to glow a very exciting colour. What is that colour? What does this colour mean to you at this time? It is an activation that your Soul has created to show you what you have asked to see. Come up to that door and again remember that you are standing there in the energy of your Soul. The Light is all around you and you feel very safe. You are also with your Spiritual Teacher who has come to assist you and, if you have invited me along, you will feel my presence and my love surrounding you as well.

If you are willing, open the door and walk in. At first it may be a little misty inside. It is very much like the dawn in the morning when there is mist all around and you can't see anything very clearly. See with your inner eye that the mist is the same colour as the door itself was and it swirls softly all around you, gently touching you as you move through it. There seems to be a lovely golden path beneath your feet so you just trust that your Soul has put that path there and walk along it through the mist, feeling its friendly presence all around you. You keep walking on this golden path with your Soul and your Teacher until you begin to see that the mists are thinning.

You see a landscape before you. Use your imagination to see it more clearly. What is the landscape like? Does it have a horizon? Is there a beautiful countryside with mountains and valleys? Is there a city or village in the distance? Perhaps there is something completely different. Simply allow it to be whatever is presented to you by your inner *wisdom. Look around. Remember, your imagination is a very powerful tool. Add some colour and detail here now. Paint the landscape and be creative. You have seen pictures of many periods in history, and the ones you believe that you haven't seen, your Soul will show you. It remembers all your adventures. Ask your Soul to help you get this picture into focus.*

Begin to walk through the landscape. Try to see it, to feel it, to experience it. Notice any smells or sounds in the air around you. At first, you may see many people or no one at all. You notice that the golden path is still before your feet. If you keep walking, you will get to where you need to go, so trust in your own purposeful movement forward. Keep looking around. You are also here to have some enjoyment, you know. You can keep asking for things to be more concrete and there must be many questions you would like to ask. Aren't you curious about what people are wearing? You might want to know if the land is healthy and happy or if it bleak and depleted. Let your curiosity guide you. Now your path will lead you to a place, and you can feel that it is important for you. In fact, the path now seems to come to an end. Notice where you are now. Look around. This is your destination.

Aha! There is a significant looking person here. If you are having trouble seeing them clearly, use more imagination. Ask for support from your Soul, and you can also say, "Vywamus, give me some of your clarity. I want to see better." Now blink your eyes and look again. Is that a man or a woman? Sometimes you will find an interesting energy that doesn't look very human if you have gone back very far, perhaps to a place other than Earth. Usually it's another human being you will see, a man or a woman. Well, look. Are they short or tall, fat or thin? What colour of hair and complexion do they have? What are they doing? Are they very active or do they seem to be very quiet? This is the life, this is the person that you have come to see.

At this point, I suggest that you make yourself more visible to this person. It will be very much for them as it is for you when a person comes to talk to you in your dreams. You know that in your dreams you are very receptive and you are perhaps more ready to listen to a strange being than you are in your waking state. If you don't know how to do this, ask your Soul. Just say, "Soul I want to be visible now." You probably are going to want to ask your Soul to be visible too. It can be very useful to you at this point. The Soul is a convincing and inspiring presence. See that the Soul and you are becoming visible and you can be seen a little distinct from the Soul. This person is seeing both of you now, you, just the way you look today, and your Soul the way you see it. You might see that the other person is looking up and says, "Well, who are you?" You should now introduce yourself. This is the natural and polite thing to do in such a situation, don't you agree? So tell the person who you are, what your name is, where you live and what year it is that you live in. Introduce your Soul as well and explain that the Soul has created you both. You may be surprised to notice that this person isn't very excited or upset, but this is because it is like a dream for them.

Now it is your turn to ask questions. I'm sure you are becoming very curious. You might begin by asking, "Who are you? I have come to find out all about your life. Are you doing well? Do you have a problem?" I suggest that you ask many questions. Channel yourself speaking to this one and channel this one's answers, please. Are they in trouble? Are they doing wonderfully well? Ask those important questions. You are the actor. You get into one role and then the other role, giving them both voices. If you are a good actor, they will both have different voices that will fit their characters and appearances. It is like a play. Ask to have some interaction between yourself, your past persona and your Soul. With the assistance of the imagination, this process can be a very exciting and very tangible learning experience.

After you have had a full discussion with this other expression of Self, you will have a very good idea of their situation. The next thing you will want to do is to ask the Soul, "How did this come about? What happened? Is there a pattern here? Tell me Soul, how did this one get into this situation? Were there choices that could have been different? What is going on here?" Look now, your Soul is smiling very wisely and saying to you, "Of course. You see there is a pattern here because there was a lesson that we wanted to learn in this life." Ask, "What was the lesson? I don't think we got it right in this life, because this situation doesn't seem very clear." Let the Soul tell you what the lesson was. You might also say to the Soul, "Why did this person make the choices they made? They don't seem to be enjoying this situation very much. They don't seem to have learned the lesson that was created there for growth. Why did they not understand?" In some cases, you will notice that the past personality has talked about another person that may be involved in its life very deeply. If you find that they are having a struggle with another person or a group of people, you might want to ask the Soul, "Who are these other ones and why do they seem to be interfering or struggling with this previous personality here? How did they get involved?" These are very important questions and the Soul has all the answers if you will allow and assist it to speak through you.

Now my friends, we get to the next part. You might say to the Soul, "Well my goodness, this is quite a little mess. You know how this is affecting my present life, Soul. Why have you shown me this past life? What is here that reflects into my life today?" Bring through the Soul's answer to these very significant questions. What do the two lives have in common? Once you have discussed this with your Soul sufficiently so that you truly feel that you have an under-standing of the connectedness between this past life con-sciousness and your present life, there is a further step.

Remember, we are not just here to find out what happened and why. We are here to heal this past life and the cor-responding difficulty in the present one. We must now seek out a solution. Ask your Soul. It knows. See how the Soul smiles and says, "I am very glad you asked, because you know there was a choice. Always you can choose the higher path, the path without fear and struggle and you will still get the lesson that is here within the life. I will show you another path they could have taken." Listen now as you channel this wisdom from your Soul. You can ask your Spiritual Teacher and I, Vywamus, for greater clarity both to channel your Soul's true message and to listen to and understand what is being explained.

Well, you know what comes next, don't you? Explain to the other personality exactly what the Soul has told you. You might want to propose that you and the previous personality, together with the Soul and the Spiritual Teacher, travel back to that moment of

decision to help the past personality to choose the path that is more loving to the Self. Use some imagination here and keep asking for clarity from your Soul and from your Teacher. Locate the moment of choice, and, following the Soul's guidance, travel along the other path, the more gentle path to knowledge without struggle and pain. Do you begin to see the realization and understanding that was here in this life for which the Soul arranged? Perhaps you and this other personality will begin to see what the point was. You may begin to get realizations. Take the time now to clarify and formulate for yourself as precisely as you can the realizations that you are touching into as you work with this past life persona and its connection into your present life. It might even be quite helpful to discuss with all the beings present in the exercise at this moment what you have discovered. Be sure to share it with this previous incarnation of Self as this will assist in resolving the conflict and balancing the energies of the past.

There is one more thing. You know you are going to have to give a little something up, something you might not want to bring back with you into your present life, something you might want to give to the Source. Just release whatever is it that this personality and you are going to have to release before you can come into the present time completely clear on this point. Is it a feeling? Is it a belief that was incorrect? Is it simply a lack of clarity or confusion? What is it that you are going to have to let go? What don't you need any more? What should this past personality leave behind? Usually it is a false belief and a very unpleasant feeling that went with it and perhaps a judgement against yourself for getting stuck in this way. Look now, have you got some baggage that you don't want to bring into the present again with you? Once you know what it is that you need to let go, see before you a great violet flame that your Soul is creating. Reach gently into your energetic structure and see what is willing to release. Allow whatever it is, be it false beliefs, confusion, judgements against yourself or pain, loss, sorrow, grief and anger to move out into the Light of your conscious acceptance and love. You may wish to see it is a mass of dark coloured material that you are allowing to be cleansed and balanced within the violet transmutational flame that your Soul is holding present for you. See it being completely consumed and transmuted into Light.

Invite your past personality to experience this same releasing and transmuting of anything it wishes now to heal within the violet flame. As you both do this, you might like to say aloud, "I release this pain and misunderstanding. I do not need it. Dear Source, please assist me to transmute

it into Light and to integrate it within my being as understanding and self acceptance." See the sparks from the violet
flame pour upward in your channel to the Source, carrying
any smoke or darkness that is there right into the bright,
white Light. You may even see in your imagination that a
great hand of white Light reaches down and gathers in all
the released energy and makes a beautiful explosion like
fireworks in a dark sky, lighting everything up.

See that sparks of beautiful Light come spiralling and dancing down your golden channel, down over you and your past
personality. Look what is happening. The Light is trigger-
ing you both and you are turning into beings of Light,
shimmering, moving, and dancing in its brilliance. You put
out your arms and you say to this other one that is becoming
Light, "Bring your strength, your wisdom, understanding
and your experiencing to me now. Come into my life, come
forward and help us express our true divine nature upon the
Earth now. You will enjoy this. Your talents are needed."
What are those talents that this one has that you would like
to bring forward to aid you in your present life? How can
this one serve Earth? What is its understanding? Pause
and consider this. Perhaps you might ask your Soul.

When you have an answer, speak a clear invitation within
your heart. Call to this past one to join Self in the Now, to
join with you and the Soul in joyous participation within the
Divine Plan. See that you both are moving points of Light
and that you begin to blend your energies, flowing together,
in Light. You begin to feel yourself embracing, accepting
and integrating the strengths and the abilities of this past
personality into Self. You both flow into the energy and
Light that is the Soul, feeling yourselves becoming one
together in the heart of the Soul.

Now, your Soul and your Spiritual Teacher walk back with
you through the landscape, down the golden path until you

come back through the door by which you entered. Walk together up the bright and beautiful corridor that you passed through when you began this journey. Move along, feeling your heart filled with joy and understanding. You come again through the first door into the heart centre. You relax, floating in the Light of the Soul, in your beautiful column of Light, safe, joyous and much more complete. You may wish to pause for a time and consider and discuss with the Soul and your Spiritual Teacher what you have seen and experienced and its significance for your present life. Take as long as you need to feel complete with the process.

When you are ready, begin to allow the channelled energy that is within your structure to gently flow away from the top of your head and throughout your whole body into the root chakra area at the base of the spine. Release it now through the feet into the Earth. Feel it flooding away like water. See it as bright Light touching into the core of the Earth. See a beautiful, emerald green/gold Light flowing up your column of Light and touching into the Source. You are a complete channel of love and Light, a connection between the Earth and the Source. You open and receive the love, Light and nurturing that is here for you, that you have created with your courage and your love. Rest comfortably in this energy until you feel yourself fully present throughout your physical structure. I thank you, for as you have released this within yourself, you have helped to release it within the mass consciousness of humanity and within the Earth itself. This is a beauteous service to Self, to the planet, to humanity and to the Divine Plan.

I salute you in love and Light,
Vywamus

BOOKS PUBLISHED BY LIGHT TECHNOLOGY PUBLISHING

Title	No. Copies	Total
Acupressure for the Soul	$11.95	$
Arcturus Probe	$14.95	$
Behold a Pale Horse	$25.00	$
Cactus Eddie	$11.95	$
Channeling: Evolutionary . . .	$ 9.95	$
Color Medicine	$11.95	$
Forever Young	$ 9.95	$
Guardians of The Flame	$14.95	$
Great Kachina	$11.95	$
Keys to the Kingdom	$14.95	$
Legend of the Eagle Clan	$12.95	$
Living Rainbows	$14.95	$
Mahatma I & II	$19.95	$
Millennium Tablets	$14.95	$
New Age Primer	$11.95	$
Poisons That Heal	$14.95	$
Prisoners of Earth	$11.95	$
Sedona Vortex Guide Book	$14.95	$
Shadow of San Francisco Peaks	$ 9.95	$
The Soul Remembers	$14.95	$
Story of the People	$11.95	$
This World and the Next One	$ 9.95	$
Robert Shapiro/Arthur Fanning		
Shining the Light	$12.95	$
Shining the Light — Book II	$14.95	$
Shining the Light — Book III	$14.95	$

Title	No. Copies	Total
Shining the Light — Book IV	$14.95	$
Robert Shapiro		
ETs and the Explorer Race	$14.95	$
The Explorer Race	$25.00	$
Arthur Fanning		
Soul, Evolution, Father	$12.95	$
Simon	$ 9.95	$
Wesley H. Bateman		
Dragons & Chariots	$ 9.95	$
Knowledge From the Stars	$11.95	$
Lynn Buess		
Children of Light, Children . . .	$ 8.95	$
Numerology: Nuances . . .	$12.65	$
Numerology for the New Age	$11.00	$
Ruth Ryden		
The Golden Path	$11.95	$
Living The Golden Path	$11.95	$
Dorothy Roeder		
Crystal Co-Creators	$14.95	$
Next Dimension is Love	$11.95	$
Reach For Us	$14.95	$
Hallie Deering		
Light From the Angels	$15.00	$
Do-It-Yourself Power Tools	$25.00	$
Joshua David Stone, Ph.D.		
Complete Ascension Manual	$14.95	$

Title	No. Copies	Total
Soul Psychology	$14.95	$
Beyond Ascension	$14.95	$
Hidden Mysteries	$14.95	$
Ascended Masters	$14.95	$
Vywamus/Janet McClure		
Aha! The Realization Book	$11.95	$
Light Techniques	$11.95	$
Sanat Kumara	$11.95	$
Scopes of Dimensions	$11.95	$
The Source Adventure	$11.95	$
Prelude to Ascension	$29.95	$
Leia Stinnett		
A Circle of Angels	$18.95	$
The Twelve Universal Laws	$18.95	$
All My Angel Friends	$10.95	$
Where Is God?	$ 6.95	$
Happy Feet	$ 6.95	$
When the Earth Was New	$ 6.95	$
The Angel Told Me . . .	$ 6.95	$
Color Me One	$ 6.95	$
One Red Rose	$ 6.95	$
Exploring the Chakras	$ 6.95	$
Crystals For Kids	$ 6.95	$
Who's Afraid of the Dark	$ 6.95	$
The Bridge Between Two Worlds	$ 6.95	$

Continued on following page

BOOKS PRINTED OR MARKETED BY LIGHT TECHNOLOGY PUBLISHING

	No. Copies	Total
ACCESS YOUR BRAIN'S JOY CENTER	$14.95	$
AWAKEN TO THE HEALER WITHIN	$16.50	$
A DEDICATION TO THE SOUL/SOLE	$9.95	$
EARTH IN ASCENSION	$14.95	$
GALAXY SEVEN	$15.95	$
INNANA RETURNS	$14.00	$
IT'S TIME TO REMEMBER	$19.95	$
I WANT TO KNOW	$7.00	$
LIFE IS THE FATHER WITHIN	$19.75	$
LIFE ON THE CUTTING EDGE	$14.95	$
LOOK WITHIN	$9.95	$
MAYAN CALENDAR BIRTHDAY BOOK	$12.95	$
MEDICAL ASTROLOGY	$29.95	$
OUR COSMIC ANCESTORS	$9.95	$
OUT-OF-BODY EXPLORATION	$8.95	$
PRINCIPLES TO REMEMBER AND APPLY	$11.95	$
SEDONA STARSEED	$14.95	$
SONG OF SIRIUS	$8.00	$
SOUL RECOVERY AND EXTRACTION	$9.95	$
SPIRIT OF THE NINJA	$7.95	$

	No. Copies	Total
TEMPLE OF THE LIVING EARTH	$16.00	$
THE ONLY PLANET OF CHOICE	$14.95	$
THE PLEIADIAN AGENDA	$15.00	$
THE TRANSFORMATIVE VISION	$14.95	$
VOICES OF SPIRIT	$13.00	$
WE ARE ONE	$14.95	$
LEE CARROLL		
KRYON—BOOK I, THE END TIMES	$12.00	$
KRYON—BOOK II, DON'T THINK LIKE .	$12.00	$
KRYON—BOOK III, ALCHEMY OF . . .	$14.00	$
KRYON—THE PARABLES OF KRYON	$17.00	$
RICHARD DANNELLEY		
SEDONA POWER SPOT/GUIDE	$11.00	$
SEDONA: BEYOND THE VORTEX	$12.00	$
TOM DONGO: MYSTERIES OF SEDONA		
MYSTERIES OF SEDONA — BOOK I	$ 6.95	$
ALIEN TIDE — BOOK II	$ 7.95	$
QUEST — BOOK III	$ 8.95	$
UNSEEN BEINGS, UNSEEN WORLDS	$ 9.95	$
MERGING DIMENSIONS	$14.95	$

	No. Copies	Total
BARBARA MARCINIAK		
BRINGERS OF THE DAWN	$12.95	$
EARTH	$12.95	$
MSI		
ASCENSION!	$11.95	$
FIRST THUNDER	$12.95	$
SECOND THUNDER	$17.95	$
ENLIGHTENMENT	$15.95	$
PRESTON B. NICHOLS WITH PETER MOON		
MONTAUK PROJECT	$15.95	$
MONTAUK REVISITED	$19.95	$
PYRAMIDS OF MONTAUK	$19.95	$
ENCOUNTER IN THE PLEIADES . . .	$19.95	$
LYSSA ROYAL AND KEITH PRIEST		
PREPARING FOR CONTACT	$12.95	$
PRISM OF LYRA	$11.95	$
VISITORS FROM WITHIN	$12.95	$
AMORAH QUAN YIN		
THE PLEIADIAN WORKBOOK	$16.00	$
PLEIADIAN PERSPECTIVES ON. . .	$14.00	$

BOOKSTORE DISCOUNTS HONORED — SHIPPING 15% OF RETAIL

SUBTOTAL: $

SALES TAX: $
(8.5% – AZ residents only)

SHIPPING/HANDLING: $
($4 Min.; 15% of orders over '30)

CANADA S/H: $
(20% of order)

TOTAL AMOUNT ENCLOSED: $

NAME/COMPANY

ADDRESS

CITY/STATE/ZIP

PHONE _____ FAX

E-MAIL

☐ CHECK ☐ MONEY ORDER

CREDIT CARD: ☐ MC ☐ VISA

#

Exp. date:

Signature:

(U.S. FUNDS ONLY) PAYABLE TO:

**LIGHT TECHNOLOGY
PUBLISHING**

P.O. BOX 1526 • SEDONA • AZ 86339
(520) 282-6523 Fax: (520) 282-4130
1-800-450-0985
Fax 1-800-393-7017

All prices in US$. Higher in Canada and Europe. Books are available at all national distributors as well as the following international distributors:

CANADA: DEMPSEY (604) 683-5541 FAX (604) 683-5521 • ENGLAND/EUROPE: WINDRUSH PRESS LTD. 0608 652012/652025 FAX 0608 652125
AUSTRALIA: GEMCRAFT BOOKS (03) 888-0111 FAX (03) 888-0044 • NEW ZEALAND: PEACEFUL LIVING PUB. (07) 571-8105 FAX (07) 571-8513